At Issue

Child Labor
and Sweatshops

Other Books in the At Issue Series:

At Issue

Child Labor and Sweatshops

Christine Watkins, Book Editor

GREENHAVEN PRESS
A part of Gale, Cengage Learning

GALE
CENGAGE Learning™

Detroit • New York • San Francisco • New Haven, Conn • Waterville, Maine • London

Christine Nasso, *Publisher*
Elizabeth Des Chenes, *Managing Editor*

© 2011 Greenhaven Press, a part of Gale, Cengage Learning.

Articles in Greenhaven Press anthologies are often edited for length to meet page require-ments. In addition, original titles of these works are changed to clearly present the main thesis and to explicitly indicate the author's opinion. Every effort is made to ensure that Greenhaven Press accurately reflects the original intent of the authors. Every effort has been made to trace the owners of copyrighted material.

Cover Image copyright © Images.com/Corbis.

LIBRARY OF CONGRESS CATALOGING-IN-PUBLICATION DATA

Child labor and sweatshops / Christine Watkins, book editor.
    p. cm. -- (At issue)
    Includes bibliographical references and index.
    ISBN 978-0-7377-4874-1 (hardcover) -- ISBN 978-0-7377-4875-8 (pbk.)
  1. Child labor. 2. Sweatshops. I. Watkins, Christine, 1951-
  HD6231.C4546 2010
  331.3'1--dc22

                         2010012649

Printed in the United States of America
2 3 4 5 6 7 14 13 12 11 10

Contents

Introduction

An estimated 218 million children between the ages of five and seventeen work as child laborers throughout the world. International treaties have defined child labor as all economic activity for children younger than twelve years of age, any work that undermines health or education for those between the ages of twelve and fourteen years, and all "hazardous work" (such as that involving exposure to toxic chemicals, continuously lifting heavy loads, or working with dangerous tools) for children younger than eighteen years of age. Almost every country prohibits child labor to some extent, yet past experiences have proved that simply banning child labor does not guarantee the health and safety of children. As Natasa Rovasevic put it in the article "Child Slavery: India's Self-Perpetuating Dilemma" for the 2007 *Harvard International Review*, "Moral imperative dictates a ban on child labor, but what of the child who will fall asleep hungry without his day's wages? . . . Labor is tantamount to survival for a vast majority of child workers." It would seem that poverty is the root cause of child labor, and therefore the main focus should be on eliminating poverty. But on second glance, it turns out to be a little more complicated.

The link between poverty and child labor has been established through numerous studies; experts maintain that child labor itself is the catalyst that perpetuates the cycle of poverty, however. It goes like this: Child laborers—with no money or time away from work for schooling—remain uneducated into adulthood, capable of performing only menial, low-paying tasks, a circumstance that necessitates their own children becoming laborers to help support the family, thus continuing the succession of child labor and poverty generation after generation. Another factor is that child labor reduces the demand for adult employment, which further suppresses the economy.

So, how is it possible to break this devastating cycle? International organizations, researchers, and policy makers believe the answer is education. Education means "freedom, liberty, development, life, and future for millions who are trapped in servitude," as Kailash Satyarthi, founder of the Global Campaign for Education, said in a 2006 speech to the Global Task Force on Child Labor and Education. "Imparting education and elimination of child labor are two sides of the same coin. One cannot be achieved without the other."

Educating children is no easy task, however. In 1989 the United Nations General Assembly adopted the Convention on the Rights of the Child, which asserts that all children throughout the world have the right to an education and requires governments to ban child labor when it interferes with a child's education. But such a law is difficult to enforce when most impoverished families need the immediate economic benefit from their children's labor far more than the future reward from education, or when parents cannot afford the cost of school. In other words, when families must choose between putting food on the table and educating their children, providing food usually wins despite any law demanding otherwise.

"What the children actually need is motivation and some incentive to attend school regularly," writes Shridhar Naik in his 2008 Chowk.com article "Child Labor—Legislation Alone Not Enough." Naik goes on to suggest, "An initiative to be considered is some form of stipendiary or financial support to cover minimum expenses, plus decent meals." Pulitzer Prize winners Nicholas D. Kristof and Sheryl WuDunn agree and consider "bribery" to be a smart strategy for expanding education. In their book *Half the Sky*, Kristof and WuDunn describe an antipoverty program, Oportunidades, organized in 1995 by the deputy finance minister of Mexico. The program pays families cash grants ranging from ten to sixty-six dollars a month to keep their children in school and to have regular medical checkups. "In essence, Oportunidades encourages poor families to invest in their children, the way rich families already do, thus breaking the typical transmission path of poverty from generation to generation. . . . The program is now widely copied in other developing countries, and even New York City is experimenting with paying bribes to improve school attendance." Approximately one quarter of Mexican families benefit from Oportunidades, and it has become one of the most admired antipoverty programs in the world.

Many domestic and international organizations, including the U.S. Department of Labor, the World Bank, the United Nations, and the International Labor Organization, recognize that education is the only permanent and self-sustaining path toward eliminating child labor, and by extension poverty. They also recognize that for compulsory education to be successful in low-income countries, policies and programs must work within the prevailing social and economic conditions. Such innovative programs are already showing positive results in China, Thailand, Mexico, and Brazil; and the Global Task Force on Child Labor and Education aims to achieve universal primary education by 2015.

The existence of child labor and sweatshops is an impassioned and challenging topic. The authors in *At Issue: Child Labor and Sweatshops* discuss various legal, ethical, and practical aspects that surround this important global issue.

1

Child Labor Harms Children

Foundation Intervida

Foundation Intervida is a nondenominational, nonpartisan, and nongovernmental organization in special consultative status with the United Nations Economic and Social Council. Active in Latin America, Asia, and Africa, the foundation has as its objective to improve the living conditions of the world's most disadvantaged populations.

Research has shown that the risks associated with labor adversely affect children to a much larger degree than adults, often resulting in irreversible damage to children's physical and mental development. The agriculture sector—the largest sector of employment—exposes children to dangerous instruments and highly toxic and carcinogenic substances. The estimated one million children who work in mines often suffer from respiratory illnesses such as emphysema, and young workers in other sectors can be exposed to lead or to benzene, a product that causes brain damage and leukemia. Despite such documentation, child labor—often hidden from general knowledge—continues to exist throughout the world.

Unacceptable forms of child labor exploitation exist and persist, but these are particularly hard to investigate given their hidden, illicit, or even criminal nature. Although there is diverse information, data, and documentation on child labor, considerable gaps still exist when trying to understand the various forms and conditions in which children work, as ac-

Alfonso Hernández, *Exploited Lives: Child Labor Exploitation*, Barcelona, Spain: Fundación Intervida, 2008. © Fundación Intervida 2008. Reproduced by permission.

knowledged by the ILO [International Labour Organization] itself. This is especially true for the worst forms of child labor, which due to their intrinsic nature, are often hidden from public scrutiny. The worst forms of child labor are those which involve slavery, debt bondage, trade, sexual exploitation, the use of children in drug trafficking and armed conflicts, and hazardous work.

The children who do these jobs are exposed to the same working conditions which adults are exposed to, and sometimes worse. However, their physical and psychological characteristics make children more vulnerable than adults in these types of activities. Studies by the ILO estimate that each additional hour of work weekly increases the probability that children suffer from work-related injuries or illnesses.

From a physical standpoint, children are not conditioned to withstand long hours of monotonous and exhausting work.

Harm to a Child's Development

Health and safety risks in the workplace are related to the nature of the work itself (for example, if this involves an intrinsically dangerous manufacturing process), to ... contact with harmful agents or substances, and to exposure to harsh working conditions. It is often the case that the workplace represents a combination of chemical, physical, biological, and psychological risks, and that the harmful effects of these, beyond being cumulative, are actually increased.

It has been shown that the effects of work on children's health may be far more serious than on the health of adults, irreversibly damaging their physical and mental development, with serious repercussions in the future. For example, carting heavy loads or adopting unnatural postures may deform or damage their developing bodies. Children are more sensitive

11

than adults to the effects of radiation and chemical products, and are less resistant to illness. They are also more physically and psychologically fragile than adults, and living and working in a work environment oppresses them and leaves long-lasting psychological scars.

From a physical standpoint, children are not conditioned to withstand long hours of monotonous and exhausting work. Their capacity for concentration is less than that of adults. Their bodies tire before adults' do, given an excessive consumption of energy, and a large majority of children suffer from nutritional deficiencies, which means they are less resistant to disease. Likewise, children are especially susceptible to work accidents, [as] they are unaware of the dangers present and do not know which precautions to take on the job; as such they are likely to suffer more serious accidents than adults.

Therefore, when it comes to children, it is necessary to go beyond the relatively limited concept of labor risks as it is applied to adults, and understand that child development is also involved.

Mortality caused by pesticide intoxication is greater than that caused by other child illnesses, such as malaria, tetanus, diphtheria, polio, and whooping cough, combined.

Harm from Working in Agriculture and Fishing

In the majority of countries, agriculture, including fishing and mining, is the largest sector of employment. As such, it is not surprising that it is also the sector which accounts for the majority of child labor worldwide. The ILO estimates that nearly three fourths of child laborers work in the agricultural sector—that is over 163 million children. Despite the fact that in some cases this work may not be considered dangerous, it may become so to the extent that the children are working long days, carrying heavy loads, working with chemical substances or dangerous instruments, or are subject to some type of abuse (whether this be physical, sexual, mental, or emotional).

Child labor in the agricultural sector was one of the most studied forms of child labor in the rapid evaluations undertaken by the ILO-IPEC [International Program on the Elimination of Child Labor] project to investigate the worst forms of child labor. Evidence of child labor was found in the following sectors: sugarcane (Bolivia, El Salvador), horticulture (Ecuador, Tanzania), tobacco (Lebanon, Tanzania), tea (Tanzania), coffee (Tanzania), and fishing (El Salvador). The children who work in agriculture worldwide are in contact with potentially dangerous machinery and biological and chemical agents. They may work on tasks such as mixing, carrying, or applying pesticides, fertilizers, or herbicides, some of which are highly toxic and carcinogenic. Contact with pesticides is more dangerous for children than for adults and is responsible for increased risks of cancer, neuropathies, neurological disorders, and anomalies of the immune system.

In agricultural exploitations and plantations, children often come into contact with organic dust. According to data from Sri Lanka, mortality caused by pesticide intoxication is greater than that caused by other child illnesses, such as malaria, tetanus, diphtheria, polio, and whooping cough, combined.

Muro-ami [reef-hunting] fishing, which obliges children to dive at sea without protection or adequate material, is very common in Asia, especially in Burma, the Philippines, Indonesia, and Thailand. Children fish, jumping on the coral reefs to scare the fish and force them into their nets. Each fishing ship employs up to 300 children between 10 and 15 years old, who are recruited from nearby villages. The divers set the nets several times a day, which means that the children may spend up to 12 hours a day in the water. Each year, dozens of adolescent divers die. They may be attacked by predators (eels, sharks, barracudas, poisonous sea snakes, etc.), they may drown or rupture an eardrum, or they may suffer from the effects of decompression or other mortal accidents, due to the strong . . . pressure.

Harm from Labor in Mining

[Although] the ILO includes mining in the same category as agriculture and fishing, this activity deserves its own section, given its particular harshness and its existence in various countries. This refers to child labor in the small mines of many African, Latin American, and Asian countries. It is estimated that one million children currently work in mines and quarries in [more than] 50 countries in Asia and South America. Children work long hours, without adequate protection, specialized clothing, or prior training, and in humid environments with extreme temperatures. Among associated risks, it is important to emphasize that contact with harmful dust, gases, and vapors provokes respiratory illnesses and may lead to silicosis, pulmonary fibrosis, asbestosis, and emphysema within a few years. Child miners also suffer from extreme physical tension and exhaustion, as well as ocular deformities and serious lesions caused by falling objects. Those who work in gold mines suffer from the toxic effects of mercury.

Young workers have a greater propensity to lose hearing capacity due to high noise levels.

In the quarries of Peru or Guatemala, children are obliged to break stone alongside their parents, gathering a cubic meter [35 cubic feet] of stone fragments for which they are paid 8 euros, three times less than what an adult receives. In Guate-

tory problems, as have been observed in the handicraft sector in the Philippines, Kenya, and Tanzania.

Solvents and glues represent an element of neurotoxicity. As such, children should not work with these substances, which are also used in the hides and leather industry. Many metallic elements contain lead and mercury, and aniline colorants are carcinogenic, which is why these should not be used by children in workshops where they dye wool for making rugs, or in the treatment of leather for shoes, where these colorants are often used.

Children are ... particularly sensitive to lead ... on construction sites, in the crystal and glass factories, and in car radiator repair workshops.

The benzene used to produce glues, gums, or rubber products, paints, and oils is another [substance] which is highly dangerous for the human organism. Its inhalation may produce drowsiness, nausea, and a loss of consciousness, and prolonged exposure to this product has effects on the medulla [lower half of the brain stem] and may cause anemia and leukemia. Children who work in automobile repair shops and gasoline stations are regularly exposed to benzene.

According to the United States Agency for Toxic Substances and Disease Registry, another highly carcinogenic material for human beings is asbestos. Children may be exposed to asbestos in mining, on construction sites, and in brake repair workshops. Asbestos fibers can cause cancer and asbestosis, a chronic lung disease produced by the inhalation of asbestos fibers. The fibers penetrate the lungs and irritate the lung tissue, inflaming it and provoking, after a few years, pulmonary fibrosis (thickening and scarring of the lung tissue). Twenty years may go by [between] the time of exposure to the asbestos fibers and the time [when] the illness begins.

Children are also particularly sensitive to lead, to which they are often exposed on construction sites, in the crystal and glass factories, and in car radiator repair workshops.

Harm from Labor in the Informal Urban Sector

Child workers, especially those who live and work in the street, are extremely vulnerable to the worst types of exploitation and may become involved in more serious types of child labor, such as drug trafficking or commercial sexual exploitation.

The informal sector [comprises] a large variety of economic activities and occupations, both legal and illegal. These activities tend to offer lower levels of income and security than formal sector jobs, and also tend to concentrate themselves in urban areas (although there also exist examples of informal work sectors in rural areas, such as in Nepal). In many developing countries it is estimated that the informal sector contributes to an important percentage of the gross national product, as is the case in Tanzania, where this reaches 32 percent. With the exception of boys and girls who work as apprentices in mechanic workshops, or those who work processing fish, for example, the majority of informal work done by children takes place in streets, parks, markets, and dumps.

In this context, child workers in the informal sector may be classified into two categories: those who work and live in the street, and those who work in the street but live in their homes or with relatives. If is difficult to determine the exact number in each category, but the children who live and work in the street seem to represent a greater percentage.

Some countries in which children work in the street include Guatemala, El Salvador, Romania, Tanzania, Turkey, and Nepal, but there are also documented cases of children working in dumps and markets in many other countries, such as Madagascar, Brazil, Kenya, Nigeria, South Africa, and India, to name a few.

Violence, both general and sexual, is one of the most serious and terrifying problems which working children face.

The children who live and work in the street are in an especially precarious situation. Extreme poverty, the lack of a decent home, the lack of support on the part of public social services, domestic violence, or difficulties in educating children are only some of the factors which create a situation of indigence and the phenomenon of "homeless children." In the United States alone it is estimated that there are 1.3 million homeless children, who have lived in the street at least once during the course of a year.

Harm from Working in Domestic Service

Domestic service is very common among children in many developing countries, and employers in urban areas often recruit children from rural areas through families, friends, or other relations. [Although] the majority come from extremely poor families, many of these children are abandoned, orphaned, or come from single parent homes. According to a survey of children working in domestic service in Togo, 24 percent of [them] are orphans.

Violence, both general and sexual, is one of the most serious and terrifying problems which working children face, and domestic service workers constitute one of the groups most exposed to this type of violence.

It is not known how many children work in domestic service, given that by definition this is a hidden activity, but it is certainly widespread, especially among girls. For example, the ILO estimates that there are more than 2 million children working in domestic service in South Africa, 559,000 in Brazil, 250,000 in Haiti, 200,000 in Kenya, 264,000 in Pakistan, and 100,000 in Sri Lanka. It is also estimated that some 700,000 children work in domestic service in Jakarta, the capital of Indonesia, alone, that 300,000 work in Dhaka, Bangladesh, and that 150,000 work in Lima, Peru.

The majority of children working in domestic service are between 12 and 17 years old, although in some cases children no older than 5 or 6 years have been found in service.

Working hours tend to be long. The Domestic Service Workers Union in Zimbabwe reports working days ranging from 10 to 15 hours long. According to a survey conducted in Morocco, 72 percent of children begin working before seven in the morning and 65 percent do not go to bed before eleven at night. There is also alarming evidence of physical, mental, and sexual exploitation among adolescents and young women working in domestic service.

2

Child Labor Causes More Harm to Girls than Boys

International Labour Office

Founded in 1919, the International Labour Organization (ILO) works to advance decent employment opportunities, social justice, and internationally recognized human and labor rights for people worldwide. The people who are employed by the organization are known as the International Labour Office.

The worst forms of child labor—such as slavery, prostitution, and hazardous work—urgently need to be abolished, and special attention should be devoted to the plight of girls. Statistics show that more girls than boys are physically abused in domestic work, spend more total hours working and thus spend fewer hours in school, and are more vulnerable to sexual abuse and prostitution.

The ILO's [International Labour Organization's] Conventions and Recommendations, along with the United Nations Convention on the Rights of the Child, provide an important legal framework for addressing issues of child labour and for ensuring that girls receive special attention.

An ILO Convention is an agreement under international law entered into by States and international organizations. Once a member State ratifies a Convention, it undertakes to accept its terms and to apply it in law and in practice. The State must, if necessary, adopt new laws and regulations or modify existing legislation and practice in order to apply the Convention.

International Labour Organization, *Give Girls a Chance: Tackling Child Labour, a Key to the Future*, Geneva, Switzerland: International Labour Organization, 2009. Copyright © 2009 International Labour Organization. Reproduced by permission.

An ILO Recommendation is an instrument that is not open to ratification but which lays down general or technical guidelines to be applied at the national level.

Approximately 53 million girls were estimated to be in hazardous work.

Girls Need Special Attention

With the adoption of ILO Convention No. 182 in 1999, a global consensus was reached on the need to eliminate the worst forms of child labour. The Convention targets such practices as the use of children in slavery, forced labour, trafficking, debt bondage, serfdom, prostitution, pornography, forced or compulsory recruitment for armed conflict, illicit activities and various forms of hazardous work. Each State that ratifies Convention No. 182 must, as a matter of urgency, take immediate and effective measures to secure the prohibition and elimination of the worst forms of child labour. Article 7 (e) of ILO Convention No. 182 stipulates that the special situation of girls must be taken into account.

Convention No. 182 calls for programmes of action to eliminate child labour, while accompanying Recommendation No. 190 stresses that such programmes should aim at giving special attention to younger children, the girl child, the problem of hidden work situations in which girls are at special risk and other groups of children with special vulnerabilities or needs. In determining the hazardous nature of work referred to in Convention No. 182, consideration should be given to work which exposes children to physical, psychological or sexual abuse.

An ILO Global Action Plan on the Worst Forms of Child Labour was endorsed in 2007 and pursues the goal of eliminating all the worst forms of child labour by 2016. Among the areas identified for action in the Plan is the need for attention to the special situation of girls. . . .

Approximately 53 million girls were estimated to be in hazardous work identified as one of the *worst forms of child labour*. Of these, 20 million were [younger] than twelve years old.

Reliable estimates on the extent of the worst forms of child labour other than hazardous work (for example, commercial sexual exploitation of children, forced and bonded labour, etc.) are difficult to obtain, but specific studies on the subject show that the majority of children involved are girls. . . .

More Girls than Boys Work in Household Services

Domestic work for an employer in a third-party household raises particular concerns in the area of child labour and is considered one of the worst forms of child labour in many countries. This is because of its frequently hidden nature and the regular reports of abuse of children in domestic work. The data . . . show that the overwhelming majority of child domestic workers are girls.

Employment hours are important because they determine the time that is available to attend school, do homework and benefit from rest and leisure. The average hours of boys and girls in employment are quite similar, though working boys in the 5–14 range have slightly longer hours (20.2 hours per week for boys versus 19.2 hours per week for girls). However, as will be seen later, the hours that girls spend on domestic work in their own homes mean that their total working time (in employment and at home) is on average greater than that of boys.

More than 35 per cent of working boys and girls below the age of 15 are in employment for 21 hours or more hours per week. At such levels of work it becomes increasingly diffi-cult for children to maintain effective participation in educa-tion. . . .

In all the countries surveyed, girls worked more hours per week than boys.

The difference between girls and boys in terms of their in-volvement in unpaid household services is greatest in sub-Saharan Africa (44 per cent), followed by Latin America (29 per cent), transitional and developed countries (15 per cent) and Asia and the Pacific (8 per cent).

Overall, the percentage of girls aged between 5 and 14 who are working is 15 per cent higher than that of boys. The engagement of both boys and girls in household services in-creases as they grow older. In the 15–17 age group the in-crease is almost twice as high for girls as it is for boys, rising by 20 percentage points as against 11 among children aged 5 to 14.

While the analysis of hours in employment referred to earlier showed that boys and girls work roughly the same hours, the differences were more noticeable when comparing the intensity of "household chores" by sex. In all the countries surveyed, girls worked more hours per week than boys.

It is important to note that the proportion of girls be-tween 5 and 11 years old who are engaged in household chores for 28 hours or more is twice as high as for boys, and about three times as high among children aged between 15 and 17 years.

Longer Work Hours Diminish School Attendance

School attendance rates vary significantly according to whether children undertake an economic activity only, an economic activity combined with household chores or household chores only. The lowest attendance rates were among girls [engaged only] in an economic activity (61.3 per cent), [whereas] girls involved in both an economic activity and household chores had an attendance rate of 71.3 per cent. This apparent paradox suggests that children combining an economic activity with household chores devote fewer hours to the former than do those engaged exclusively in an economic activity and that it is the long hours spent in regular employment that are most detrimental to school attendance. Girls who were not involved in any economic activity but were occupied only in household chores had an attendance rate of 81.5 per cent.

As the number of hours devoted to household chores increases, the capacity of children to attend school diminishes. Girls working more than 21 hours a week are particularly affected.

The drop in school attendance is sharper as the hours in employment increase. Thus, the average school attendance rate of economically active children working for 28 hours or more per week is only 62 per cent of that of those working fewer than 14 hours. The pattern is similar both for boys and for girls.

Girls work quite significantly more than boys in unpaid work in their own households.

While it is important not to draw global conclusions solely on the basis of data taken from the survey of sixteen countries presented here, the data do provide an important indication of the pattern of work among girls and boys engaged in both economic activities and unpaid household services. Some of the key points are:

- If economic and non-economic activities are taken together, the statistics indicate that girls work more hours than boys. This confirms the need for a comprehensive framework for analysing all the forms of work performed by children and for assessing the implications of those activities.

- There is little difference between the hours that boys and girls spend working in economic activities, but girls work quite significantly more than boys in unpaid work in their own households.

- More than 25 per cent of boys and girls below the minimum age of employment who were employed in economic activities worked for 28 hours or more per week. At this level it is very difficult to engage in education.

- Ten per cent of girls aged 5–14 years performed household chores for 28 hours or more per week. This is twice as high as the percentage of boys.

- The average school attendance rate of girls who performed household chores for 28 hours a week was 25 per cent lower than that of girls who [did] so for fewer than 14 hours a week. . . .

Vulnerable young girls are sometimes subjected to beatings and brutal treatment, as well as to verbal or sexual abuse.

The Particular Difficulties of Domestic Work

Domestic work can be hazardous both because of the tasks undertaken and because of the conditions of work. Regular tasks performed by young girls include kitchen duties (involving work with knives and hot pans), laundry and cleaning (sometimes entailing the use of toxic chemicals), helping out in the employer's business, undertaking agricultural tasks for the family and child minding. Many girls work very long hours, often more than 15 hours daily, and they are always on call. The heavy workload and lack of rest can pose a serious problem, and many girls experience stress and fatigue due to lack of sleep.

A study in Nepal found that a large proportion of child domestic workers are illiterate, though this is not the case everywhere. Some girls are unclear about the wages they are entitled to, their hours of work, whether . . . they are authorized to attend school and other conditions of work. Domestic work is generally not well paid, and sometimes not paid at all. In Haiti, for example, many children work in exchange for food and lodgings. In South Africa, one study found that boys are more likely to be paid for domestic tasks than girls, who spend much longer on such work.

Girls Are More Vulnerable to Abuse

Because the work is undertaken in private households, government services, trade unions and NGOs [nongovernmental organizations] often have difficulty reaching and protecting girls in domestic service. When girls are allowed by their family to spend long hours in other people's households, they are completely under the control of the employer or relative, who may not necessarily have the girl's best interests at heart. With no system of regulating or enforcing children's rights, vulnerable young girls are sometimes subjected to beatings and brutal treatment, as well as to verbal or sexual abuse. Consistent subjection to abuse inevitably leads to a loss of self-esteem and thus the abuse becomes self-perpetuating, with girls accepting a low status and being unable to challenge the situation. . . .

ILO Convention No. 182 identifies the use of children in prostitution and pornography as one of the worst forms of child labour. [Although] it is impossible to know the true extent of the problem, the ILO has estimated that at least 1.8

million children are exploited in commercial sex or pornography worldwide, the vast majority of them being girls. . . .

Trafficking of girls from rural areas has been identified as a major problem. Very often girls are lured into prostitution in cities, having travelled from rural areas in the belief that they had a chance of employment in legitimate work. Practices such as sending daughters to live and work with members of the extended family can contribute to the vulnerability of girls. A domestic labour environment that becomes abusive can result in the girls leaving the family in which they work. If they believe that they cannot return home or have nowhere to go, such girls are then immediately more vulnerable to individuals who prey on young people in difficult situations.

Some girls become involved in commercial sexual exploitation simply to survive. Very often alternative survival strategies (getting married, entering domestic employment, living with relatives) have failed. Others may have experienced physical or sexual abuse, lack of protection, emotional neglect or abandonment.

Victims of trafficking and sexual exploitation are often subjected to extreme violence, and they may require gynaecological treatment as well as therapeutic counselling for trauma. Sexually exploited girls may experience unwanted pregnancies, and [they] are in danger of contracting HIV/AIDS [human immunodeficiency virus/acquired immunodeficiency syndrome] and other sexually transmitted diseases.

3

Legislation Helps Prevent Child Labor

Tom Harkin

Tom Harkin is a United States senator from Iowa. He is currently the chairman of the Senate Committee on Health, Education, Labor, and Pensions and is a longtime leader in the fight to end abusive child labor.

Abusive child labor practices must end. Such practices are not only morally wrong, they are also bad economic policy for all nations involved. Legislation that penalizes countries for exploiting children, that sets standards for nonabusive labor practices, and that monitors the enforcement of such rules is an effective tool in preventing, once and for all, abusive child labor worldwide.

Abusive child labor is a profound moral evil. It is also bad economic policy, and it undermines the development goals of emerging nations. When a child is exploited for the economic gain of others, the child loses, the family loses, the country loses, and the world loses. Nations that engage in abusive child labor make bad trading partners. A nation cannot achieve prosperity on the backs of its children. There simply is no place in the global economy for the slave labor of children.

During my three decades in the U.S. Congress, I have witnessed firsthand the horrors of abusive child labor in many

Tom Harkin, "U.S. Legislative Initiatives to Stop Abusive Child Labor," *eJournal USA*, May 2005, pp. 17–19.

countries. Once you see children toiling in fields and factories, children who are beaten and starved, children who live without love or even basic care, you can't help but be passionately committed to ending this scourge.

Historical Legislation to Reduce Child Labor

To reduce child labor internationally, Congress has developed a wide range of tools, both legislative and nonlegislative, to combat abusive child labor practices. For example, Section 1307 of the Tariff Act of 1930 forbids the importation of goods made with forced or indentured labor. In 2000, this act was amended to ensure that the statute also applied to goods made with forced or indentured *child* labor.

The Trade and Development Act of 2000 was a great step forward in the fight against abusive child labor in the developing world. Under this act, countries eligible to receive trade preferences under the Generalized System of Preferences are obliged to implement their commitments on abusive child labor. The Office of the United States Trade Representative is required by law to conduct a yearly review of countries receiving these benefits to determine, among other things, whether they are implementing their commitments under International Labor Organization (ILO) Convention 182 to eliminate the worst forms of child labor.

Under Convention 182, for the first time, countries reached agreement on the definition of the worst forms of child labor. This definition includes all forms of slavery, the trafficking of children, debt bondage, and recruiting children for prostitution, pornography, and the production of or trafficking in drugs. Also included in the definition is work that by its very nature is likely to harm the health, safety, or morals of children. Convention 182 was negotiated in 1999. As of April 2005, 153 of the 178 ILO member countries, including the United States, had ratified the convention. In ratifying the convention, these nations, including many developing countries, have agreed to eliminate abusive child labor as an "urgent" matter.

In the Trade Act of 2002, the law that contains the trade promotion authority for U.S. trade negotiators, I attempted to include a requirement that the elimination of the worst forms of child and slave labor be a principal negotiating objective in all U.S. trade negotiations. Regrettably, in the final form of the 2002 act, this objective was seriously weakened, stating only that U.S. negotiators may raise the issue of abusive child labor with trading partners.

In 1999, I introduced the Child Labor Deterrence Act [the legislation was not passed into law]. I will soon reintroduce this bill, which instructs the president to work with our trading partners to secure an international ban on trade in products made with abusive child labor. If passed, such legislation would prohibit the importation of manufactured and mined goods that are produced by abusive child labor into the United States. It also would require the development and maintenance of a list of foreign industries that use abusive child labor. Companies violating the prohibition against importing these products would be subject to stiff penalties. Although this legislation stalled in 1999, I was able to amend the Trade Act of 2000 to ensure that the statute also applied to goods made with forced or indentured child labor.

Rehabilitation consists of removing children from abusive work and providing them with education or vocational training.

Actions to Eliminate Abusive Child Labor in the Chocolate Industry

Parallel with these legislative initiatives, I have pursued voluntary, nonlegislative approaches—most prominently, the

Harkin-Engel Protocol to eliminate abusive child labor and slave labor in the chocolate industry.

In 2001, Representative Eliot Engel, from the state of New York, joined me in crafting an initiative to eliminate abusive child and slave labor in the chocolate industry in West Africa. The Harkin-Engel Protocol prescribes a comprehensive, six-point, problem-solving approach, along with a time-bound process for credibly eliminating the use of abusive child and slave labor in the production of cocoa beans and derivative cocoa products in the countries of West Africa. The protocol specifically provides for the development of global industry-wide standards and independent monitoring, reporting, and public certification. Industry has agreed to certify that cocoa used in chocolate or related products has been grown and processed in West Africa without abusive child labor.

The U.S. Congress has helped to develop a number of effective national and international legal and voluntary tools to combat and finally eliminate abusive and slave child labor.

Through the Labor, Health and Human Services, and Education Appropriations Subcommittee, I secured funding for an ILO program to monitor and rehabilitate child labor in West African cocoa fields. Rehabilitation consists of removing children from abusive work and providing them with education or vocational training. The ILO program is called the West Africa Cocoa and Commercial Agriculture Project (WACAP), which combines awareness-raising of families and communities with a child labor monitoring and feedback system that produces accurate and credible reports on child labor in West African cocoa production. Through the WACAP program, the ILO will monitor and assist approximately 80,000 children. [Although] WACAP has provided the necessary resources, the chocolate industry ultimately bears the social, moral, and financial responsibility for fully implementing the protocol.

The Harkin-Engel Protocol ensures that organized labor and other nonindustry stakeholders, along with experts on the ground in cocoa-producing countries, play an active role in working with the industry to monitor child labor practices. Representatives of the ILO; the International Union of Food, Agricultural, Hotel, Restaurant, Catering, Tobacco, and Allied Workers' Association; Free the Slaves; the National Consumers League; and the Child Labor Coalition are all part of an advisory group to help implement the terms of the protocol.

Finally, a key commitment under the protocol calls for the implementation of an industry-wide certification system by July 1, 2005.

Actions to Enforce the Legislation

In sum, the U.S. Congress has helped to develop a number of effective national and international legal and voluntary tools to combat and finally eliminate abusive and slave child labor. The challenge today is for nations, international organizations, nongovernmental groups, and industry to use these tools robustly and aggressively.

No one underestimates the scale and difficulty of the challenge ahead of us. But the moral imperative is obvious, and the economic and development arguments are compelling. It is our solemn duty—as nations, as organizations, and as human beings—to end, once and for all, the scourge of abusive child labor. It takes government, industry, and international organizations, all acting in concert, to implement these tools effectively.

4

Legislation Does Not Prevent Child Labor

Christian Parenti

An American investigative journalist, author, and lecturer, Christian Parenti has appeared on radio shows and has taught at the New College of California and at St. Mary's College in Moraga, California.

Despite international laws and campaigns by governments and human rights organizations to ban abusive child labor in the chocolate industry, child workers—many younger than age ten— continue to toil under brutal conditions. United States Representative Eliot Engel and Senator Tom Harkin introduced legislation in 2001 (known as Harkin-Engel) that mandated a child-labor-free labeling system for chocolate. Since that time, there is little evidence of compliance. Farmers need their children to work to avoid poverty, and the corrupt government of Ivory Coast would rather see high profits than improved working conditions for the poor.

Outside the village of Sinikosson in southwestern Ivory Coast, along a trail tracing the edge of a muddy fish-pond, Madi Ouedraogo sits on the ground picking up cocoa pods in one hand, hacking them open with a machete in the other and scooping the filmy white beans into plastic buckets. It is the middle of the school day, but Madi, who looks to be about 10, says his family can't afford the fees to send him to the nearest school, five miles away. "I don't like this work," he says. "I would rather do something else. But I have to do this."

Christian Parenti, "Chocolate's Bittersweet Economy," CNNMoney.com/Fortune, February 15, 2008. Reproduced by permission.

Sinikosson, accessible only by rutted jungle tracks, is a long way from the luxurious chocolate shops of New York and Paris. But it is here, on small West African farms like these, that 70 percent of the world's cocoa beans are grown—40 percent from just one country, Ivory Coast. It's not only the landscape that is tough. Working and living conditions are brutal. Most villages lack electricity, running water, health clinics or schools. And to make ends meet, underage cocoa workers, like Madi and the two boys next to him, spend their days wielding machetes, handling pesticides and carrying heavy loads.

This type of child labor isn't supposed to exist in Ivory Coast. Not only is it explicitly barred by law—the official working age in the country is 18—but since the issue first became public seven years ago [in 2001], there has been an international campaign by the chocolate industry, governments and human rights organizations to eradicate the problem. Yet today child workers, many under the age of 10, are everywhere. Sometimes they're visibly scarred from their work. In the village of Lilo, a young boy carrying a machete ambled along a road with a bandaged shin. He said he had cut his leg toiling in a cocoa patch.

Children still work in cocoa production, regularly miss school, perform dangerous tasks and suffer injury and sickness.

The big cocoa exporters—Cargill, Archer Daniels Midland (ADM, Fortune 500), Barry Callebaut and Saf-Cacao—do not own plantations and do not directly employ child workers. Instead, they buy beans from Ivorian middlemen called pisteurs and treton. These middlemen own warehouses and fleets of flatbed trucks that travel deep into the jungle to buy cocoa from the small independent farmers who grow most of the crop. But labor and human rights activists charge that Big Chocolate has an obligation to improve working conditions on the farms where so many children toil. They argue that the exporters and manufacturers bear ultimate responsibility for conditions on the farms because they exert considerable control over world cocoa markets, essentially setting what is called the farm gate price.

A Mandate Versus Protocol

The controversy came to a head in 2001, when U.S. Representative Eliot Engel (D-N.Y.) and Senator Tom Harkin (D-Iowa) introduced legislation mandating a labeling system for chocolate. The industry fought back, and a compromise was reached establishing a voluntary protocol by which chocolate companies would wean themselves from child labor, then certify that they had done so. The certification process would not involve labeling of products, but it would call for public reporting by African governments, third-party verification and poverty remediation by 2005. When none of those deadlines was met, the protocol was extended until July 2008. To turn up the heat, the U.S. Department of Labor contracted with Tulane University to monitor progress.

Tulane recently released its first report, and though the tone is polite, the picture isn't pretty. Researchers found that while industry and governments in West Africa have made initial steps, such as establishing task forces on child labor, conditions on the ground remain bad: Children still work in cocoa production, regularly miss school, perform dangerous tasks and suffer injury and sickness. The report criticized the governments of Ivory Coast and Ghana for lack of transparency. And it said the industry's certification process "contains no standards."

In some respects the situation only got worse after Harkin-Engel. From 2002 to 2004, Ivory Coast was gripped by civil war. As militias and renegade soldiers killed and raped their way across the lush interior, income from cocoa exports helped fuel the fighting. Like diamonds and timber, cocoa became a so-called conflict resource. "Blood chocolate" was providing fast cash for armed groups and creating misery for common people. Since 2004, Ivory Coast has settled into an armed peace, with French and UN troops keeping the warring factions apart. But chocolate exporters and manufacturers say the war and its aftermath have hampered their efforts to eradicate child labor.

The industry's two main trade groups, the Chocolate Manufacturers Association and the National Confectioners Association, say tens of millions of dollars have been spent on building a socially responsible cocoa sector across West Africa. But the Tulane report criticizes the industry for not providing specifics to back up those assertions. And on the ground there is little evidence anyone is paying much attention. "What protocol?" asks Ali Lakiss, the director general of Saf-Cacao, the largest cocoa exporter in Ivory Coast, which controls about 20 percent of the trade. "The farmers don't get the best price. If the cocoa price is good, then kids go to school. No money, and kids work at home."

Ivorian government officials likewise describe their efforts to stop child labor as robust, but they remain fuzzy about details. "This is our No. 1 export," says N'djore Youssouf, the technical adviser to Ivory Coast's presidential task force overseeing Harkin-Engel compliance. "This issue is taken seriously at every level of the government." But Youssouf acknowledges that remediation "has not yet begun."

Cocoa prices have been declining in recent years . . . because of corruption and a poorly planned economic liberalization.

Poverty Breeds Child Labor

Outside Sinikosson, El Hadj Madi Sankara cultivates 27 acres of cocoa, from which he usually harvests ten tons of beans, earning about $9,000 a year but remaining deeply in debt.

Sankara and his 11-year-old son, Ibrahim, are preparing a large mound of cocoa pods for processing. "I want to help my father," says Ibrahim, standing on a pile of pods, toying with his machete. "I need to learn how to be a farmer." His sentiment captures the complexity of the child-labor issue here: Typically it is poverty that compels child labor, not greedy overseers.

Soon a group of young men and boys join the work. Among them are 8-year-old twins Hassan and Hussein. The boys, the children of a neighbor, are helping Sankara make his harvest on time. Their payment won't be in cash, but in reciprocal help from Sankara's family to their father. Not one of the kids goes to school. "We're all doing a hard job," says Sankara, "but we do not get a just price."

Cocoa prices have been declining in recent years—currently about 90 cents a kilo [2.2 pounds]—because of corruption and a poorly planned economic liberalization. President Felix Houphouët-Boigny, who ran Ivory Coast from the late 1950s until the mid-1990s, borrowed heavily against his country's assets and wasted the money on megalomaniacal vanity projects, such as the world's largest basilica [church]—built in the country's desolate interior. During his reign, Houphouët-Boigny invited in hundreds of thousands of Muslim farmers from neighboring Mali and Burkina Faso to grow cocoa. These immigrants produced abundant and profitable crops, and Ivory Coast became one of the region's more prosperous and stable countries. But the newcomers were not given citizenship, identity papers or legal rights.

When the bills on Houphouët-Boigny's squandered loans came due in 1999, the government imposed fiscal austerity and liberalized the economy. Its marketing board, Caistab, was defanged, prices were deregulated and new oversight agencies and development funds were created to support the market and aid farmers hurt by lower farm gate prices. According to European Union and World Bank audits, these new government bodies now collect three times as much money from the cocoa sector, much of it from exporters, as did the old system, but they spend little on infrastructure or subsidies. In short, not much money gets past corrupt officials and down to the farmers.

Economic hard times followed, and many native Ivorians turned against the immigrants from Burkina Faso and Mali. Demagogues preached a xenophobic creed that they called Ivorité, and in 2002 ethnic tensions exploded into civil war. Now, with the front lines frozen and the armed peace holding, the many non-Ivorian cocoa workers, like those who live in Sinikosson, are trapped on remote farms. The dirt roads connecting them to the main markets are controlled by hostile, corrupt police and soldiers who threaten them with deportation or shake them down for bribes. "I've not been into the main town for four years," says Aladji Mohamed Sawadogo, the chief of Sinikosson. "The last time I tried to go I did not have enough money to pay all the bribes at the checkpoints. I am just stuck. These are the conditions in which we live."

Better Prices Make a Difference

With a wispy beard and a thin, weather-beaten face, Sawadogo looks older that the 55 years he claims. He admits that the village children work, including his own. He even allows them to be interviewed. "I'd like to be a mechanic," says one of his kids, who looks to be about 7 but says he is 11, "but I have to farm cocoa." Adds Sawadogo: "We are not happy that we ourselves live and work like this. Of course we don't want it for our children. But there is no choice."

What would make a difference? "Better prices."

Down the road from Sinikosson is the warehouse of Aboulaye Trooré, who buys the cocoa harvested in the area. "It is all going to Cargill," Trooré says, as some of his men unload 150-pound bags of cocoa from a truck.

The farmers in Sinikosson do not know that Cargill buys their beans, but other farmers in the area are on painfully intimate terms with the Minnesota company. In the town of Thoui, members of a local farmers' cooperative say that borrowing money from Cargill has trapped them in debt and forced some of them to take their kids out of school and put them to work. "There is no other way we can buy fertilizer or feed our families throughout the year," says N'guessan Norbert Walle, a former president of the cooperative.

If farmers can't pay back their debts, they risk arrest. When Walle ran the co-op, his manager was jailed, he says, on orders from Cargill. The arrested manager, Lucien Adje, a former accounting student, says he was taken to the port city of San Pedro and put in a small cell. "You had to do everything in one place—you know, urinate, defecate. I couldn't eat much, it was so filthy."

The correct procedure for collecting debts is to go to court and seize collateral, so Adje's arrest was illegal. But, as one farmer explained, "In Ivory Coast, the illegal is normal." An executive at an Ivorian export company confirmed that such arrests take place. "I don't know the specifics, but I do know that some exporters have arrested people who owe them money."

Cargill Denies Wrongdoing

Cargill denies any wrongdoing. "We have never paid for, or requested, the detention of managers or members of farmer cooperatives, and we do not support illegal detention," says company spokesman Steven Fairbairn. As for child labor, Fairbairn says the company is working hard to fix the problem: "We require that all our direct suppliers of cocoa beans in West Africa sign a statement acknowledging that they understand that we are committed to the elimination of the worst forms of child labor in the cocoa supply chain. If suppliers are found to be employing such practices, their contracts are subject to termination."

But Cargill has yet to terminate any contracts over the issue of child labor. And it and other exporters say they don't have an obligation to pay higher prices. "We are just an intermediary," says Saf-Cacao's Lakiss, "between the farmers and international markets in London."

Hershey (HSY, Fortune 500), like other major chocolate firms, signed the Harkin-Engel protocol and maintains it is working. "The protocol's value is seen in measurable progress on the ground," says Kirk Saville, a Hershey spokesman. "It has created greater community awareness of child welfare issues and increased incomes for family farms and access to education."

But Hershey has no direct role in implementing reforms in Ivory Coast. Instead, the protocol required the industry to create a foundation to oversee certification. That body is the International Cocoa Initiative, or ICI, headquartered in Geneva and funded by the chocolate industry to the tune of about $2 million a year. The foundation began its work in Ivory Coast in 2003, and it claims to have six pilot projects underway there. "We are doing high quality, scalable work," says Peter McAllister, ICI's executive director. "We've not yet had a significant effect, but it's a journey." He is unfazed about the looming July 2008 deadline: "We don't see it as ending in 2008. Our process works, and we're committed for the long term."

But the foundation has only one staff member in Ivory Coast, Robale Kagohi, and his activities appear limited. "One of the main problems is the moral poverty of the people," says, Kagohi, sitting in a tiny office in the basement of a building in Abidjan that houses a corporate law firm. "That is why we are spending so much time on education." He explains that the anti-child-labor campaign has so far favored "sensitization"—workshops with local officials, police and farmers to explain that child labor is wrong and that if it continues,

Ivory Coast will be shut out of world cocoa markets. On the roads there are billboards urging people to say no to child labor.

Impoverished farmers in Ivory Coast say loss of markets would also hurt them and their children.

Education or Intimidation?

Farmers describe these efforts as more akin to intimidation than to education. "People are worried that America will not buy our cocoa anymore," says Julien Kra Yau, director of a farmers' cooperative in Thoui. "That would be very bad." Adds the co-op's treasurer, Raymond Kouasse Kouadio: "It would be a total catastrophe!"

ICI's other work involves helping a nongovernmental organization called the Movement for Education, Health, and Development, or Mesad, provide accommodation and education to homeless street children. But no children from the cocoa sector were staying at the shelter on a visit last fall, and the group's director, Kouakou Kouadio Watson, says ICI has supported only eight underage former cocoa workers, who lived at the shelter for periods of between one and four months. The shelter is a squalid mess, smelling of urine, and a few filthy children sleep on the concrete floors.

The industry's evident lack of compliance with Harkin-Engel puts everyone involved in a difficult position. New coercive legislation requiring "child-labor-free" labeling could cause trouble for the large cocoa exporters and chocolate manufacturers if there were boycotts of non-labeled chocolate. But impoverished farmers in Ivory Coast say loss of markets would also hurt them and their children. Since the idea was first floated in 2001, the chocolate industry has taken the same position: Labeling "would hurt the people it is intended to help," says Susan Smith, a spokeswoman for the Chocolate Manufacturers Association and the World Cocoa Foundation.

A more effective way to combat child labor would be for the government . . . to invest some of the revenue it gets from high taxes on cocoa exporters in education and social services.

There is fair-trade chocolate on the market, but it accounts for no more than 1 percent of global supply—and the movement has little traction in Ivory Coast. A more effective way to combat child labor would be for the government of Ivory Coast to invest some of the revenue it gets from high taxes on cocoa exporters in education and social services to help poor farmers. But the government of Ivory Coast is ranked among the most corrupt in the world by Transparency International, a nongovernmental watchdog group. And [the government] seems happier making excuses than changes.

Angeline Kili, head of the government body tasked with financing and regulating the cocoa sector, blames farmers from Burkino Faso and Mali for whatever child labor violations may be occurring. "They need labor, so they have kids working, sometimes with the bad consequences," she says. "Sometimes they traffic children. Child labor wasn't a big problem, but it became a big problem recently. You have to remember, all cocoa farmers worked as kids. Our president worked on a farm with his parents for no money."

Representative Engel, for one, isn't happy with the lack of progress. He and Senator Harkin plan to travel to Ivory Coast soon on a fact-finding mission of their own. "We have given the industry plenty of time," Engel says. "I am not prepared to give another extension."

5

Child Labor Laws Should Be More Strictly Enforced

Sally Greenberg

Sally Greenberg is the executive director of the National Consumers League, a private nonprofit group that advocates for social and economic justice in the workplace.

Efforts by the Department of Labor (DOL) to enforce laws that protect working children are dangerously inadequate. Although the number of children working in the United States has grown to approximately 3.2 million, the numbers of child labor investigations and hours spent researching violations have decreased dramatically in the last several years. For example, children under the age of fifteen working in agriculture account for an estimated 75 percent of all work-related deaths in that age group, yet in 2006 only twenty-eight DOL investigations occurred. In an effort to protect young people from serious injury and death in the workplace, Congress must devote more investigative time, impose higher penalties for violations, and eliminate special exclusions for agriculture workers.

The National Consumers League [NCL] believes that . . . much more can and must be done to better protect our young people from hazards and dangers they confront in the workplace.

Every 10 days in America, a young person is killed at work. Every day, more than 100 young workers under the age of 19 are seriously injured or become ill from their jobs.

Sally Greenberg, Remarks Prepared for Delivery Before the Subcommittee on Workforce Protections of the U.S. House Committee on Education and Labor, U.S. House Committee on Education and Labor, September 23, 2008.

My testimony today focuses on the U.S. Department of Labor, or DOL's, poor enforcement of the federal child labor laws, and I will make recommendations about reforms I would like to see at DOL to strengthen protections for working children. I will also make recommendations for legislative reforms that we believe Congress should consider to help to protect our young people from hazardous work conditions. . . .

Let me start by saying that the NCL very much supports the notion young people can learn and grow by working, as long as they are placed in a jobs that are appropriate and safe. We wish to focus, however, on workplace settings and jobs that are risky or dangerous for young people and what can be done to correct the loopholes in the law that expose youngsters to these workplace hazards.

Much of my testimony is based on the findings of two reports on DOL's child labor enforcement released by the Child Labor Coalition and published by the National Consumers League, one in June 2005 and the other in September 2006, as well as more recent data on the same topic. . . .

Child Labor Investigations and Penalties Are Negligible

What these reports make clear is that enforcement of the child labor law is no longer a high priority for DOL.

Here is a quick overview that shows why this is so.

First, the number of child labor investigations by DOL has declined drastically. For example, there was a 48 percent decline from 2004 to 2006—2,606 child labor investigations in 2004, but only 1,344 in 2006. If we look back more than two years, the story is even worse. The number of child labor investigations conducted in 2006—1,344—was the lowest in the last 10 years for which we have data, and may be the lowest in many decades.

Second, the time spent investigating child labor also declined: 58,220 hours in 2004, but only 48,005 hours in 2006. If we look back more than two years, the story is even worse. For example, from 2001, when the Wage [and] Hour division spent 73,736 hours doing child labor investigations, to 2006, the time devoted to child labor investigations plummeted by 35 percent. The 48,005 hours spent by DOL in 2006 investigating child labor violations may sound like a lot of time, but based on our calculations, this is roughly the equivalent of 28 full-time employees doing child labor investigations exclusively. There are an estimated 3.2 million working children in the United States, according to the federal government. In other words, each of these 28 DOL child labor investigators is in effect responsible for assuring a safe and healthy work environment for about 115,000 youth workers.

[Department of Labor] has almost no child labor enforcement in agriculture.

Third, the penalties that DOL imposes are too low to provide sufficient deterrent to companies hiring underage workers. [Although] the law imposes a maximum penalty of $11,000 for each violation, the average penalty in 2004 was only $718, less than 7 percent of the maximum penalty permitted. Two years later, in 2006, the average penalty was only $939, less than 9 percent of the maximum penalty. Here's a concrete example of low child labor penalties. In 2006 DOL found 29 children in six Target Corporation retail stores in New York's Hudson River Valley who had been working in jobs prohibited for children under age 18 because the work is so hazardous—operating power-driven scrap paper balers and operating power-driven hoisting equipment, like forklifts. DOL imposed a penalty of $92,400, or an average of $3,166 per child, not a lot for a multibillion-dollar corporation. Another example dates from 2005. Wal-Mart committed child labor violations affecting 85 children in 24 stores, many involving youth who did jobs that DOL has determined to be particularly dangerous, such as operating chain saws, cardboard balers, and forklifts. DOL imposed $135,540 in penalties, or an average of $1,595 per child. Given that Wal-Mart had $285 billion in annual sales, the $135,540 total penalty is a negligible amount—the equivalent of fining someone with an average salary a tiny fraction of a penny. The law says that the size of any child labor penalty that DOL imposes must take account of "the size of the business of the person charged and the gravity of the violation," but it is hard to see how DOL has done that in its investigations, given the very low amount of the average penalty imposed.

There is no deterrent effect when a large company faces a nominal penalty after permitting underage youth to perform work forbidden under [Department of Labor] regulations.

Fourth, DOL has almost no child labor enforcement in agriculture. Hundreds of thousands of children work in agriculture, yet, in 2006, just 28 of DOL's 1,344 child labor investigations—2 percent—were in agriculture. In 2005 the number of child labor investigations in agriculture was even lower—just 25. These numbers contrast sharply with earlier years. In 1999, for example, DOL conducted more than five times as many investigations in agriculture—142. What is particularly troubling about this poor enforcement record is that the risks of injury, illness, and death are greater for children working in agriculture than in any other jobs. For example, children ages 15 to 17 working in agriculture have [more than] four times the risk of fatal injury of children working in other industries. Children under age 15 working on farms account for about three fourths of all work-related deaths for that age group. As for nonfatal injuries, hospital emergency room and workers' compensation data have suggested that youth injuries in agriculture tend to be more severe than injuries in other employments.

Necessary Measures to Better Enforce Child Labor Laws

What can DOL do to assure greater protections to working children? There are several key steps DOL should take.

First, DOL needs to devote more time and effort to investigating potential child labor violations. The equivalent of 28 full-time child labor investigators for the entire United States is simply indefensible. The child labor provisions of the FLSA [Fair Labor Standards Act] are unique in that only DOL can enforce them, whereas the FLSA's minimum wage and overtime pay provisions can be enforced not only by DOL, but also by aggrieved employees represented by lawyers in court. In other words, if DOL places less emphasis on enforcing the minimum wage and overtime pay provisions, employees have another route to address the problem—a private right of action. In 2006, for example, DOL filed only 3 percent—143 of 4,207—of FLSA lawsuits in federal court. But if DOL does not enforce the FLSA's child labor provisions, then no one else can.

Second, DOL needs to impose much higher penalties than in the past. Average penalties of less than $1,000 do not provide sufficient deterrent effect. There is no deterrent effect when a large company faces a nominal penalty after permitting underage youth to perform work forbidden under DOL regulations. DOL could easily change its regulations, or even just revise its internal procedures for calculating penalties, to achieve this result. Moreover, DOL should take employers who commit repeat child labor violations to court to get an injunction barring future violations, as the FLSA authorizes DOL to do. Any employer that violates such an injunction can be held in contempt of court and be required to pay DOL's costs of investigating and prosecuting to prove to the court that the employer has violated the injunction.

Third, DOL needs to update and strengthen its regulations that list jobs that are so hazardous that no child under age 18 (or in agriculture, under age 16) can do them. The government's premier job safety agency—the National Institute for Occupational Safety and Health, or NIOSH—issued a lengthy report [more than] six years ago [around 2002] recommending that more than half of these existing regulations be revised and that 17 new regulations be added, but DOL has acted on a paltry number of these recommendations, and adopted no changes whatsoever for agriculture, the most dangerous work environment for children. Six years of inaction, while children are maimed and injured on the job, are six years too many. DOL's refusal to protect working children by appropriately revising the hazardous orders is inexcusable.

Fourth, DOL needs to conduct targeted investigations of two industries in which child laborers may be most vulnerable to death or injury: agriculture and meatpacking. It has been nearly a decade since the Department of Labor's targeted Salad Bowl investigation found dozens of children, including many under the age of 10, helping harvest the nation's fruits and vegetables. And in the area of slaughterhouses, the recent investigation by the state of Iowa of the Agriprocessors plant in Postville, Iowa, found dozens of minors working illegally in what is often considered to be one of the worst and most dangerous jobs in America. In August, NCL spoke to an Agriprocessors child laborer who had stabbed himself in the arm while on the cutting line and had been bandaged up and told to go back to work. The young worker said he was routinely cheated out of hours of wages each week. He also said that he believed his plant supervisors knew he was too young to work in the plant but looked the other way. Given that meat processing plants tend to attract an impoverished, mostly immigrant work force, the possibility that child laborers may be employed in slaughterhouses around the nation should be investigated by U.S. DOL with vigor.

Fifth, DOL needs to publicize its child labor enforcement activities much more aggressively. The most that DOL does typically is to issue an innocuous press release, and in many instances no publicity at all is given to child labor penalty cases. This approach needs to be changed drastically to make both employers and employees much more aware of the child labor laws, and the penalties that can result for violating those laws.

Congress should mandate that child labor inspections become a greater priority of enforcement efforts.

Sixth, DOL needs to revive the Child Labor Task Force that coordinated child labor enforcement efforts between state and federal inspectors. Increased coordination and communication between state and federal inspectors should increase the efficacy of enforcement efforts.

Recommendations to Strengthen Child Labor Laws

What can this committee and Congress do to strengthen the child labor law? We have several recommendations:

First, Congress must increase funding for DOL Wage and Hour inspectors. One of the primary reasons for the lack of child labor enforcement: Wage and Hour is grossly under-staffed. [Fewer] than 750 investigators are available to go out into the field and investigate labor violations. That translates to one investigator for every 10,000 businesses. Kim Bobo, the executive director of Interfaith Worker Justice testified in Congress earlier this summer [2008] that if the ratio of investigators to businesses that existed in 1941 held today, we would have 34,000 investigators—not [fewer] than 1,000. As a first step, NCL believes the number of inspectors should be doubled and Congress should mandate that child labor inspections become a greater priority of enforcement efforts. Congress should require DOL to report on its enhanced child labor enforcement efforts not less than 18 months after funding for the additional inspectors is provided.

Second, Congress should eliminate many of the special exclusions in agriculture that permit children as young as 12 years old, and in some cases even younger, to work in the fields. It is unconscionable to allow 12-year-olds to toil in . . . 100-degree heat and be exposed to toxic chemicals and pesticides; this gaping loophole in the law should be changed. By doing so, Congress would ensure that children working in agriculture would be subject to the same protections as children working in all other jobs. We are not talking here about children who work on their own parent's farms (who are not subject to the child labor law at all), but children who work for hire on farms, such as migrant and seasonal farmworkers. Representative Lucille Roybal-Allard's Childrens Act for Responsible Employment, also known as the CARE Act, would close these shameful loopholes, leveling the playing field for hundreds of thousands of farmworker youth who are dropping out of high school in high numbers.

Third, because of the great hazards to children working in agriculture, Congress should strengthen the protections for children working on farms. Under existing law, the Secretary of Labor has the authority to declare which jobs are particularly hazardous for children, and the law provides a minimum age of 18 for such jobs—except in agriculture, where the minimum age is 16. For example, a young worker must be 18 to drive a forklift at a Wal-Mart warehouse, but that young worker could drive a forklift at a fruit and vegetable packing house at age 16—even though the dangers are very similar.

Congress should amend the law to raise the minimum age for doing particularly hazardous work in agriculture to 18, especially in view of the high incidence of deaths and injuries to children working in agriculture (as noted above). The CARE Act would remedy this problem as well.

Fourth, Congress should impose minimum penalties for child labor violations—say at $500—to make employers more likely to comply with the child labor requirements.

Child Labor Laws Should Be Repealed

Jeffrey Tucker

Jeffrey Tucker is the editorial vice president of the think tank Ludwig von Mises Institute. Tucker is also an adjunct scholar with the Mackinac Center for Public Policy and an Acton University faculty member.

Because of outdated and arbitrary child labor laws, youth today are denied valuable opportunities, such as earning an income, developing skills, and acquiring a sense of responsibility and work ethic. These child labor laws are so capricious and nonsensical that children are allowed to perform unrestricted work for state or local governments but are not allowed to work part-time in a parent's law firm, for example. The result is a blow against the freedom of choice for parents and their children, as well as a generation of ill-prepared students joining the workforce. For the benefit of society, child labor laws should be repealed.

Let's say you want your computer fixed or your software explained. You can shell out big bucks to the Geek Squad, or you can ask—but you can't hire—a typical teenager, or even a preteen. Their experience with computers and the online world is vastly superior to that of most people over the age of 30. From the point of view of online technology, it is the young who rule. And yet they are professionally powerless: they are forbidden by law from earning wages from their expertise.

Might these folks have something to offer the workplace? And might the young benefit from a bit of early work experi-

Jeffrey Tucker, "The Trouble With Child Labor Laws," InsideCatholic.com, January 22, 2008. Reproduced by permission of the author.

ence, too? Perhaps—but we'll never know, thanks to antiquated federal, state, and local laws that make it a crime to hire a kid.

Pop culture accepts these laws as a normal part of national life, a means to forestall a Dickensian nightmare [referring to conditions in author Charles Dickens's novels] of sweat shops and the capitalist exploitation of children. It's time we rid ourselves of images of children tied to rug looms in the developing world. The kids I'm talking about are [among] the most courted of all consumer sectors. Society wants them to consume, but law forbids them to produce.

A Symbol of Prosperity

You might be surprised to know that the laws against "child labor" do not date from the 18th century. Indeed, the national law against child labor didn't pass until the Great Depression—in 1938, with the Fair Labor Standards Act. It was the same law that gave us a minimum wage and defined what constitutes full-time and part-time work. It was a handy way to raise wages and lower the unemployment rate: simply define whole sectors of the potential workforce as unemployable.

Today, we are far more likely to recognize the contribution that disciplined work makes to the formation of character.

By the time this legislation passed, however, it was mostly a symbol, a classic case of Washington [D.C.] chasing a trend in order to take credit for it. Youth labor was expected in the 17th and 18th centuries—even welcome, [as] remunerative work opportunities were newly present. But as prosperity grew with the advance of commerce, more kids left the workforce. By 1930, only 6.4 percent of kids between the ages of 10 and 15 were actually employed, and 3 out of 4 of those were in agriculture.

In wealthier, urban, industrialized areas, child labor was largely gone, as more and more kids were being schooled. Cultural factors were important here, but the most important consideration was economic. More developed economies permit parents to "purchase" their children's education out of the family's surplus income—if only by forgoing what would otherwise be their earnings.

The law itself, then, forestalled no nightmare, nor did it impose one. In those days, there was rising confidence that education was the key to saving the youth of America. Stay in school, get a degree or two, and you would be fixed up for life. Of course, that was before academic standards slipped further and further, and schools themselves began to function as a national child-sitting service. Today, we are far more likely to recognize the contribution that disciplined work makes to the formation of character.

Haphazard State and Federal Laws

And yet we are stuck with these laws, which are incredibly complicated once you factor in all state and local variations. Kids under the age of 16 are forbidden to earn income in remunerative employment outside a family business. If Dad is a blacksmith, you can learn to pound iron with the best of 'em. But if Dad works for a law firm, you are out of luck.

From the outset, federal law made exceptions for kid movie stars and performers. Why? It probably has something to do with how Shirley Temple led box-office receipts from 1934 [to] 1938. She was one of the highest-earning stars of the period.

If you are 14 or 15, you can ask your public school for a waiver and work a limited number of hours when school is not in session. And if you are in private school or home school, you must go ask your local Social Service Agency—not exactly the most welcoming bunch. The public school itself is also permitted to run work programs.

This point about approved labor is an interesting one, if you think about it. The government doesn't seem to mind so much if a kid spends all nonschool hours away from the home, family, and church, but it forbids them from engaging in private-sector work during the time when they would otherwise be in public schools drinking from the well of civic culture.

The legal exemption is also made for delivering newspapers, as if bicycles rather than cars were still the norm for this activity.

Here is another strange exemption: "youth working at home in the making of wreaths composed of natural holly, pine, cedar, or other evergreens (including the harvesting of the evergreens)." Perhaps the wreath lobby was more powerful during the Great Depression than in our own time?

Oh, and there is one final exemption, as incredible as this may be: federal law allows states to allow kids to work for a state or local government at *any* age, and there are no hourly restrictions. Virginia, for example, allows this.

The exceptions cut against the dominant theory of the laws that it is somehow evil to "commodify" the labor of kids. If it is wonderful to be a child movie star, congressional page, or home-based wreath maker, why it is wrong to be a teenage software fixer, a grocery bagger, or ice-cream scooper? It makes no sense.

Employers will tell you that most kids coming out of college are radically unprepared for a regular job.

Loss of Valuable Experience and Freedom of Choice

Once you get past the exceptions, the bottom line is clear: full-time work in the private sector, for hours of their own choosing, is permitted only to those "children" who are 18 and older—by which time a child has already passed the age when he can be influenced toward a solid work ethic.

What is lost in the bargain? Kids no longer have the choice to work for money. Parents who believe that their children would benefit from the experience are at a loss. Consumers who would today benefit from our teens' technological know-how have no commercial way to do so. They have been forcibly excluded from the matrix of exchange.

Child-labor laws were and are a blow against the freedom to work and a boost in government authority over the family.

There is a social-cultural point, too. Employers will tell you that most kids coming out of college are radically unprepared for a regular job. It's not so much that they lack skills or that they can't be trained; it's that they don't understand what it means to serve others in a workplace setting. They resent being told what to do, tend not to follow through, and work by the clock instead of the task. In other words, they are not socialized into how the labor market works. Indeed, if we perceive a culture of sloth, irresponsibility, and entitlement among today's young, perhaps we ought to look here for a contributing factor.

The law is rarely questioned today. But it is a fact that child-labor laws didn't come about easily. It took more than a hundred years of wrangling. The first advocates of keeping kids out of factories were women's labor unions, who didn't appreciate the low-wage competition. And true to form, labor unions have been reliable exclusionists ever since. Opposition did not consist of mining companies looking for cheap labor, but rather parents and clergy alarmed that a law against child labor would be a blow against freedom. They predicted that it would amount to the nationalization of children, which is to say that the government rather than the parents or the child would emerge as the final authority and locus of decision-making. . . .

In every way, the opponents were right. Child-labor laws were and are a blow against the freedom to work and a boost in government authority over the family. The political class thinks nothing of legislating on behalf of "the children," as if they are the first owners of all kids. Child-labor laws were the first big step in this direction, and the rest follows. If the state can dictate to parents and kids the terms under which teens can be paid, there is essentially nothing they cannot control. There is no sense in arguing about the details of the law. The critical question concerns the locus of decision-making: family or state? Private markets or the public sector?

Youth Lack Lessons in Productivity

In so many ways, child-labor laws are an anachronism. There is no sense of speaking of exploitation as if this were the early years of the industrial revolution. Kids as young as 10 can surely contribute their labors in some tasks in ways that would help them come to grips with the relationship between work and reward. They will better learn to respect private forms of social authority outside the home. They will come to understand that some things are expected of them in life. And after they finish college and enter the workforce, it won't come as such a shock the first time they are asked to do something that may not be their first choice.

We know the glorious lessons that are imparted from productive work. What lesson do we impart with child-labor laws? We establish early on who is in charge: not individuals, not parents, but the state. We tell the youth that they are better off being mall rats than fruitful workers. We tell them that they have nothing to offer society until they are 18 or so. We convey the impression that work is a form of exploitation from which they must be protected. We drive a huge social wedge between parents and children and lead kids to believe that they have nothing to learn from their parents' experience. We rob them of what might otherwise be the most valuable early experiences of their young adulthood.

In the end, the most compelling case for getting rid of child-labor laws comes down to one central issue: the freedom to make a choice. Those who think young teens should do nothing but languish in classrooms in the day and play Wii at night will be no worse off. But those who see that remunerative work is great experience for everyone will cheer to see this antique regulation toppled. Maybe then the kids of America can put their computer skills to use doing more than playing *World of Warcraft*.

7

Child Agriculture Workers Need Stronger Labor Laws

Benjamin Hess

Benjamin Hess is the director of communications for the Association of Farmworker Opportunity Programs, which advocates to improve the quality of life for migrant and seasonal farm workers in the United States.

Experts consider agriculture to be one of the most hazardous industries for workers—especially for young laborers. For example, exposure to pesticides is widespread in fields and orchards and has been linked to cancer, neurological problems, respiratory problems, and developmental problems; children are more vulnerable than adults to these risks because their bodies are smaller and their organs are still developing. Field investigations have also found that children as young as nine years old sometimes work ten to twelve hours a day in blistering weather conditions, exposing them to heat exhaustion, dehydration, and skin cancer. Furthermore, farm work often involves carrying heavy loads and constant bending over, which contribute to physical and developmental injuries. For these and other reasons, the U.S. government must do more to strengthen child labor safeguards in the agriculture industry.

Sweat beads down Sergio's face as he toils in a south Texas onion field. He picks onions with the skill and pace of an adult, yet he is only ten years old. Sergio wears a sleeveless

Benjamin Hess, "Introduction; 2: Working Conditions; 6: A Call to Action: Federal Legislation, Regulatory Enforcement, and Research," Children in the Fields: An American Problem, May 2007. © 2007 by Association of Farmworker Opportunity Programs. Reproduced by permission.

shirt and shorts, and the May sun scorches his skin. His bare feet sink into the hot earth, exposing him to harmful pesticides that have been sprayed on the soil. A [bandage] falls off his sweaty finger, revealing a gash where Sergio had cut himself earlier with his razor-sharp scissors, used for trimming the onion stalks. He has been working in the fields since age seven.

Nearby, nine-year-old Cristina works alongside five family members, including siblings and cousins. This is her second weekend in the fields, and she struggles to keep up with the others. Together, the six hope to earn $100 for a full day's work, which averages out to around $2 per hour worked.

Agriculture is considered one of the three most dangerous industries in the United States.

More than a dozen other children are working in the same field. They lean over to snip and gather onions. Exhaustion paints their faces as they carry heavy buckets to burlap sacks stationed around the field. The children earn about a penny for every pound of onions picked.

Because Sergio and Cristina are less than 12 years old, their employer may be violating the federal child labor law by allowing them to work. Most of the other children, however, appear to be at least 12 years old; such children can legally work in agriculture, except during school hours, with their parents' permission or with their parents on the same farm. For children who are at least 14 years old, the only restriction is that they cannot work during school hours.

The Dangers from Working in Agriculture

Hundreds of thousands of children work as hired labor in America's fields and orchards. These children are among the least-protected of all working children. Since 1938, exemptions in the federal child labor law—the Fair Labor Standards Act, or FLSA—have excluded child agricultural workers from many of the protections afforded to almost every other working child. Agriculture is considered one of the three most dangerous industries in the United States. For agricultural jobs that are determined by the Secretary of Labor to be particularly hazardous for children, federal law imposes a minimum age of 16. The minimum age for hazardous work in all other industries is 18. Furthermore, in the case of jobs that are not determined to be particularly hazardous, federal law sets the standard minimum age in agriculture at 14 years, whereas the standard age limit in all other sectors of the economy is 16 years. Moreover, in agriculture there are numerous exceptions that enable children as young as ten to work legally on farms. Despite overwhelming evidence from public agencies and private organizations that these agricultural workplaces endanger children, Congress maintains the legal discrimination in the FLSA. This inequity allows youth working on farms to perform back-breaking labor for long hours and in extreme conditions at ages less than 14, when the very same law forbids children this young from working in an air-conditioned office.

Since 1997, the Association of Farmworker Opportunity Programs (AFOP) has advocated for stronger federal child labor laws through its Children in the Fields campaign. It has partnered with the Child Labor Coalition (CLC), the National Consumers League, and other concerned parties to publicize the plight of this hidden population. It has used its extensive network of member agencies to inform the public and advocate for federal legislation that would strengthen the child labor safeguards in agriculture so that they are just as protective as those in all other industries. AFOP has conducted field investigations that have uncovered children as young as nine working in the fields. Most Americans still envision farms as safe, nurturing places. The Children in the Fields campaign has shown that the myth of the agrarian idyll does not extend to the children of America's migrant and seasonal farmworkers. . . .

The Danger from Pesticides

Seventeen-year-old Gloria was picking oranges when she began to complain of nausea, dizziness, blurred vision and stomach cramps. The orchard had been sprayed with pesticides the day before. No warning signs had been posted.

Recent studies have demonstrated the greater health risks that pesticides pose for children. The Natural Resources Defense Council's 1998 report on the perils of pesticide exposure for children noted that children are at higher risk than adults because their bodies and organs are more vulnerable and they "are disproportionately exposed to pesticides compared with adults due to their greater intake of food, water, and air per unit of body weight." The 2002 NIOSH [National Institute for Occupational Safety and Health] report noted that the incidence of acute occupational pesticide-related illness in youth is 1.71 times that of working adults aged 25 to 44 years. In July 2006, scientists at the Wake Forest University School of Medicine released a report showing that children of immigrant farmworkers in North Carolina had higher levels of organophosphate insecticides in their urine samples than children who did not live on farms. Although the researchers could not conclude that the exposure was enough to damage the children's health, lead researcher Thomas Arcury said, "Because we don't know how much is safe, we must assume, as a precaution, that no level is safe. Efforts to reduce the exposure of these children to pesticides must be redoubled."

Currently, the Environmental Protection Agency's (EPA) regulations prohibit farmworkers from reentering a sprayed area for a specific time interval except under very limited circumstances. The EPA's Worker Protection Standard bases its established reentry intervals (REIs) on a body weight of 154 pounds, except for those pesticides that might affect a fetus, in which case the EPA uses a body weight of 132 pounds (considered the average for a pregnant female of child-bearing age). The 154-pound body weight is considered the average for a male adult, which means that children take potentially harmful risks when they enter fields after they have been sprayed with pesticides, even if they follow the REIs....

In March 2000, the GAO [General Accounting Office] released a report calling for numerous changes that would better protect child farmworkers. According to the report, over 75 percent of all pesticides in the United States—950 million pounds a year—are used in the agricultural sector. Children have a high skin to body weight ratio and are in a more rapid stage of development, which makes them more vulnerable than adults to pesticide exposure. According to the Pesticide Action Network North America (PANNA), organophosphate and carbamate pesticides—two common types—"are linked to cancer, neurological problems (including Parkinson's disease), respiratory problems, and developmental problems." Farmworkers also suffer a disproportionately high number of cases of dermatitis, which may be connected to pesticide exposure.

A study in the April 2003 issue of the *American Journal of Public Health* examined pesticide-related illnesses among youth workers. From 1993 to 1998, the researchers identified 333 acute illnesses among teen workers ages 15 to 17. Sixty-four percent of the sicknesses occurred in agricultural workers. At least 18 youth were sickened despite following the Worker Protection Standard reentry requirements. "Because these acute illnesses affect young people at a time before they have reached full developmental maturation, there is also concern about unique and persistent chronic effects," the study's authors wrote. "The FLSA and the Worker Protection Standard should be reviewed and appropriately revised to ensure that workers younger than 18 are protected against toxic pesticide exposures."

An Increased Risk of Cancer

Furthermore, Canadian researchers published a study in the *Annals of the New York Academy of Science* in October 2006 that drew a link between women farmworkers and breast cancer. According to the study, women with breast cancer were nearly three times more likely to have worked on farms—many at a young age, when breast tissue is believed to be more vulnerable to toxins—than women in the control group. "Agents present in agricultural settings may make a woman more susceptible to breast cancer, especially if she is exposed to these agents early in her life," co-principal investigator Dr. James Brophy said. He also noted, "The major cancer studies going on in North America . . . are focusing specifically on farms in the rural states, because there has been this seemingly large increase in cancer in this normally healthy population."

There may not yet be clear evidence of the exact extent to which children are more vulnerable than adults to the harmful effects of pesticides, but there is little debate about children's greater vulnerability. The EPA acknowledged in March 2003 that children ages 3 to 15 may be three times more likely to develop cancer after exposure to certain pesticides than adults. In August 2006, the EPA concluded a ten-year investigation on the health effects of pesticides with a recommendation to eradicate 3,200 uses and modify 1,200 uses of organophosphate and carbamate pesticides, which together make up approximately 45 percent of the total pesticide applications in the United States. Nevertheless, the EPA has faced harsh criticism, including objections from its own employees, for failing to implement more stringent restrictions that would better protect agricultural workers and their families. In a letter published on May 24, 2006, leaders of three unions representing EPA employees criticized the EPA for endangering public health by allowing the ongoing use of potentially harmful pesticides. The letter emphasized the dangers that children face from pesticide exposure, noting, "The children of farmworkers, living near treated fields, are also repeatedly exposed through pesticide drift onto outdoor play areas and through exposure to pesticide residues on their parents' hair, skin, and clothing."

Although the EPA acknowledges the negative health impact of pesticides on children, it has been slow to react and defensive when its policies are questioned. In November 2003, DOL [Department of Labor] stated that the EPA would address concerns raised by the International Labor Organization regarding pesticide dangers to child farmworkers, but no public statement has been made since. Inexplicably, despite its own admission that children probably face a greater risk than adults, the EPA continues to use the 154-pound body weight to determine its reentry intervals.

The EPA should devise unique REIs for child farmworkers that compensate for their lower body weight and particular susceptibility to pesticides. Moreover, Congress should amend the child labor law to raise the minimum age for particularly hazardous work in agriculture from 16 to 18 years. Additionally, the U.S. Department of Labor should amend its child labor regulations so that pesticides and other dangerous chemicals of all toxicity categories are covered, not just Toxicity Categories I and II. There is a need for increased research on the subject, and it should be given the highest priority, in view of the importance of protecting children.

Children reported working in fields where the drinking water would run out, no water was provided, or the only beverages available were overpriced beers and sodas.

The Danger from Environmental Conditions and Lack of Sanitation

Seventeen-year-old Martin died after harvesting melons in the hot sun for 4 hours. He was taken by ambulance to a hospital after complaining of a headache, nausea, and difficulty breathing. He died because his body overheated.

Farm labor is often carried out in excruciating weather conditions that add an extra burden to the grueling tasks that farmworkers perform. Farmworkers regularly work for 10 to 12 hours a day in 100-degree temperatures under a blistering sun. These circumstances can lead to sunstroke, skin cancer, heat exhaustion, dehydration, and other sun- and heat-related illnesses. No national statistics on the number of heat-related farmworker fatalities are available, but during the summer of 2005, six farmworkers died in heat-related incidents in California and three others died in North Carolina. The EPA and DOL's Occupational Safety and Health Administration (OSHA) have acknowledged that children are more vulnerable to heat stress than adults.

During field investigations in May 2003, AFOP found children as young as nine and ten years old working in Texas onion fields, where temperatures reached the mid-90s, although it was only late spring. Two of the principal causes of skin cancer are unprotected or excessive exposure to harmful UV [ultraviolet] radiation—which is strongest between 10 A.M. and 4 P.M.—and severe sunburns as children. According to the Arizona Department of Health Services, 80 percent of a person's lifetime sun exposure occurs before the age of 18, and a single bad sunburn in childhood can double the risk of developing skin cancer in the future. AFOP staff noticed that many child farmworkers wore clothing that left much of their skin exposed to the sun.

In 2000, a Human Rights Watch study on child farmworkers found that "nearly all of the children interviewed" had worked on farms where sanitation requirements were not met. Children reported working in fields where the drinking water would run out, no water was provided, or the only beverages available were overpriced beers and sodas. Aside from placing an unfair economic burden on farmworkers, these two beverages adversely affect workers' health and safety, since carbonated and alcoholic beverages fail to replenish fluids and alcohol can impair workers' ability to safely operate tools and machinery. Furthermore, farmworkers who might drink water from irrigation ditches or other contaminated sources as a last resort risk illnesses such as dysentery and typhoid fever.

[Because] children are still developing physically, their exertion often places a greater stress on their bodies, with serious long-term consequences.

Around half of the teens interviewed by Human Rights Watch had no access to handwashing facilities. This increases their risk of harm from pesticides, especially since many farmworkers eat lunch on-site. Human Rights Watch noted that some workers would wash in contaminated irrigation ditches. In fact, sometimes water from irrigation ditches was provided to workers so they could wash their hands. Human Rights Watch interviewed Art Morelos, a compliance supervisor with Arizona's Occupational Safety and Health Division, who commented, "Occasionally farm labor contractors will get water from the ditches or drainage canals and put it in a container as water for the employees to wash their hands with." Water from irrigation canals often contains harmful chemicals, waste material, and parasites. Morelos also reported that a lack of toilet facilities was the "biggest complaint in the fields."

Regulations issued by OSHA require all farms (except for certain small farms) to provide workers of all ages with access to drinking water, hand-washing facilities, and toilets, but weak enforcement has resulted in these services often not being provided. Improved enforcement and stricter penalties would push agricultural employers to extend these basic protections to all farmworkers, including children. Farmworkers should also receive training about how to detect and protect themselves from heat exhaustion, dehydration, and skin cancer. . . .

The Danger of Musculoskeletal Injuries

Farm work often involves constant bending over, carrying heavy items, and repetitive motions during long work hours, which contribute to musculoskeletal injuries. [Because] children are still developing physically, their exertion often places a greater stress on their bodies, with serious long-term consequences. Adolescents also undergo growth spurts, which may decrease flexibility and increase their susceptibility to a variety of musculoskeletal injuries, such as bursitis, tendonitis, sprains, and carpal tunnel syndrome.

A 2004 study on the risk of low-back disorders among youth farmworkers published in the *Journal of Agricultural Safety and Health* revealed that "the magnitude of several work-related factors . . . for many farm activities were equal to or greater than those associated with high injury risk jobs previously assessed in industrial workplaces." In 2001, researchers Larry Chapman and James Meyers wrote, "Emerging data suggest that agriculture faces a near epidemic of musculoskeletal disorders." Several studies demonstrate that agricultural workers are among the most susceptible to musculoskeletal injuries in the United States. One study estimates that more than 60 farmworkers per 1,000 suffer from musculoskeletal disorders, with direct health care costs in excess of $167 million. The Migrant Clinicians Network also alludes to studies that indicate that musculoskeletal disorders are the chief cause of injury among farmworkers. The National Agricultural Workers Survey (NAWS) found that 24 percent of California farmworkers had suffered from at least one musculoskeletal injury in 2003 to 2004.

To protect child farmworkers from long-term injuries, DOL should develop federal ergonomics standards governing those farm jobs with the highest incidence of musculoskeletal disorders, such as hand harvesting, pruning, and hand weeding. The standards should provide youth farmworkers engaged in these activities with frequent breaks and limit the number of hours that children can perform these jobs. In 1997, California became the first state to implement ergonomics standards in agriculture, but other states have been slow to follow its example. . . .

The U.S. government must act swiftly to protect child farmworkers from dangerous and exploitative labor that has long-term adverse consequences for their physical and mental development. All children should have the right to enjoy their childhood. It is imperative that U.S. law be revised to ensure that this right is extended to child farmworkers.

8

Free Trade Agreements and a Global Economy Increase Sweatshops

Global Exchange

Global Exchange, an education and action resource center, works for international human rights and to limit the cost of globalization so that working people can thrive.

Free trade agreements, such as the North American Free Trade Agreement (NAFTA), allow corporations to locate in other countries. Amid today's grueling atmosphere of cost-cutting competition, many businesses are taking advantage of these agreements and are locating to countries that employ minimal labor and safety regulations. For example, in Nicaragua, Mexico, and El Salvador, workers regularly suffer physical, verbal, and sometimes sexual abuse; are exposed to toxic chemicals; and often incur workplace injuries—all while earning wages as low as twenty-eight cents an hour. The more free trade agreements that are enacted, the more corporations that can exploit sweatshop production. The result will be low wages, few opportunities, and no dignity for workers worldwide.

A decade ago [in the late 1990s], most people . . . knew about sweatshops [only] through what they had read in history books. Today, people read about sweatshops in their daily newspapers. The sweatshop, once thought to be a relic of another time, has returned with a vengeance.

Global Exchange, "Frequently Asked Questions: 'Free Trade' and Sweatshops," Global Exchange.org, October 28, 2007. Reproduced by permission.

The resurgence of the sweatshop can be directly linked to the expansion of corporate globalization. The sweatshop is both metaphor for and proof of the lawlessness and inequities of the new global economy. Every new sweatshop exposé raises new doubts about who corporate globalization is really benefiting.

The Free Trade Area of the Americas (FTAA) will drastically accelerate corporate globalization in the Americas, giving more power to multinational corporations at the expense of ordinary citizens. This will likely spread sweatshop-style production to more countries. As dog-eat-dog competition among countries increases, workers will likely see their already-low wages drop even further and their already-assaulted rights face even more threats.

What Is a Sweatshop?

There are several different ways to define a sweatshop. According to the US Department of Labor, a sweatshop is any factory that violates more than one of the fundamental US labor laws, which include paying a minimum wage and keeping a time card, paying overtime, and paying on time. The Union of Needletrades Industrial and Textile Employees (UNITE), the US garment workers union, says any factory that does not respect workers' right to organize an independent union is a sweatshop. Global Exchange and other corporate accountability groups in the anti-sweatshop movement would add to this definition any factory that does not pay its workers a living wage—that is, a wage that can support the basic needs of a small family.

In the popular mind, a sweatshop is identified with hard work. And, in fact, garment manufacturing's reliance on human labor helps explain why apparel factories are so often sweatshops.

The softness of the garments used to make our clothes, along with the complicated patterns involved, means that apparel production doesn't easily lend itself to mechanization. For more than 150 years, the sewing machine has been, and today remains, the best way of making clothes. The basic method of garment production continues to be a worker, usually a woman, sitting or standing at a sewing machine and piecing together portions of cloth. Every blouse, every pair of jeans, every T-shirt, and every pair of shoes has to be tailored by a person doing the work. Everything we wear is made by someone.

To keep labor costs low, apparel shop owners usually pay workers a "piece rate." That means workers don't get paid by the hour. Rather, their wage is based on the number of items— shirts, shoes, socks—they complete in a shift. If workers hope to earn a decent income, they have to work hard, and they have to work long. Basically, they have to sweat.

What Kinds of Abuses Do Workers Face?

Around the world, garment workers spend dozens upon dozens of hours a week at their sewing machines to make the clothes and shoes that eventually end up on retailers' shelves. Verbal, physical, and sexual abuse are common. Workplace injuries occur regularly. The wages are low. And when workers try to organize to defend their interests and assert their dignity, their efforts are invariably repressed. In country after country, the stories are hauntingly the same.

Workers at a plant in El Salvador, for example, say they are frequently required to work mandatory overtime as they sew jerseys for the National Basketball Association, according to the National Labor Committee, an anti-sweatshop group. That means they often put in 11-hour shifts, six days a week. If the workers at that factory refuse to work overtime, they lose a day's pay. Workers making jeans in Mexico say that sometimes they are forced to work all night shifts, and are prevented from leaving the factory by armed security guards.

"I spend all day on my feet, working with hot vapor that usually burns my skin, and by the end of the day my arms and shoulders are in pain," a Mexican worker, Alvaro Saavedra Anzures, has told labor rights investigators. "We have to meet the quota of 1,000 pieces per day. That translates to more than a piece every minute. The quota is so high that we cannot even go to the bathroom or drink water or anything for the whole day."

In the grueling atmosphere of desperate cost-cutting by corporations, work is accorded little value and, by extension, workers are afforded little dignity. Viewed more as production units than as people, sweatshop workers regularly suffer abuse and intimidation from factory supervisors. "They don't respect us as human beings," a Nicaraguan worker has told anti-sweatshop groups.

Verbal abuse is particularly common, and workers regularly report being harassed and bullied by shop managers. Workers who managers think are not working fast enough are usually the target of shouting and yelling. Physical abuse is also not unusual. Workers at a factory in Mexico making collegiate apparel for Reebok and Nike have said managers there regularly hit them and slap them, according to the Workers' Rights Consortium.

Sexual abuse is endemic. Most garment workers are women, the vast majority of them young women in their teens or twenties who have left their homes for the first time so that they can earn money to send back to their families.

Sweatshops don't provide real opportunities because the corporations are so determined to keep wages low.

According to Human Rights Watch, in the maquiladoras [foreign-owned factories in Mexico] along the US-Mexico border, factory managers who want to weed out pregnant workers so they can avoid having to pay maternity benefits force women workers to prove they are menstruating, a demeaning procedure that is against Mexican laws. Mandatory pregnancy tests are also common in El Salvador, and women who test positive are fired, also in violation of that country's laws.

Workplace injuries and exposure to toxic chemicals also pose a daily risk to apparel workers. To prevent workers from stealing the items they are producing, factories sometimes lock the plant's doors and windows, creating a fire hazard. In many factories, workers are not given masks to put over their noses and mouths, exposing them to [dangerous glues or tiny cloth fibers that get stuck in the lungs].

What Corporate Competition Means for Wages

Whenever a debate about corporate globalization and sweatshops arise, defenders of the status quo will almost always say: Sure a sweatshop is bad, but at least it gives people jobs they wouldn't have otherwise. The response to this short-sighted argument is: But what kind of jobs? Yes, poor people want jobs. But they also want to be treated with dignity and respect. It's always worthwhile to give people new opportunities. The problem is that sweatshops don't provide real opportunities because the corporations are so determined to keep wages low.

The shantytowns of the free trade zones and the squalid dormitories connected to garment plants reveal that a sweatshop is defined as much by the factory itself as by what surrounds the factory. That is, the corporations may have invested in their factories, but they have not invested in the workers.

In their drive to keep consumer prices low [and] sales numbers growing, and [to] post profits that will please investors on Wall Street, the US retail industry has become more ruthlessly competitive year after year. As the retailers put pressure on their subcontractor manufacturers to keep prices down, the manufacturers in turn squeeze the costs out of the workers, forcing them to work harder for less. The big losers are the workers—the people actually making the products.

According to the National Labor Committee, a worker in El Salvador earns about 24 cents for each NBA [National Basketball Association] jersey she makes, which then sells for $140 in the US. A Global Exchange investigation revealed that workers in Mexico producing jeans for the Gap earn as little as 28 cents an hour. In poorer countries such as Haiti and Nicaragua, the wages are even lower.

In their efforts to attract investment, developing countries deliberately keep their wages low. While multinational corporations often say that workers are paid the local minimum wage, the minimum wages are set at a poverty level, rarely high enough to support a family or allow a person to save for the future.

The 60 cents an hour the Salvadoran NBA seamstresses earn is only about a third of the cost of living, and even the Salvadoran government says this wage leaves a worker in "abject poverty." Likewise, the women making Gap jeans say they would have to earn about three times what they do to support their families. When Nike workers at seven of the company's subcontractor plants in Central and South America were asked about their earnings, two thirds said they didn't make enough to save or support others, according to a study funded by Nike itself.

Corporations now have more freedom than ever before to locate to whatever countries will provide the lowest wages and the loosest regulations, thereby keeping the company's costs in check.

But if the conditions and wages in sweatshops are so terrible, why do workers tolerate it? Often they don't. In countries around the world, garment workers have sought to improve their situation by trying to organize unions. Those efforts are almost always crushed. Union organizers have been beaten, thrown in jail, blacklisted, and even killed. In some countries, such as Mexico, the government often cooperates with factory owners as they try to bust organizing drives. In a few countries with strong labor histories, such as Nicaragua and the Philippines, unions are tolerated, but not in the "free trade" zones where most sweatshops are located. In these manufacturing zones, workers are expected to leave their liberty at the factory gates.

"We're not against foreign investment in Nicaragua," a worker there has told rights groups. "But we are against exploitation."

How Do Sweatshops Fit in with the Global Economy?

The signature characteristic of the new global economy is the increased mobility and flexibility given to finance capital. Corporations now have more freedom than ever before to locate to whatever countries will provide the lowest wages and the loosest regulations, thereby keeping the company's costs in check. The retail industry has taken advantage of this new dynamic like few other business sectors.

If sweatshops have become a metaphor for globalization's excesses, that's because garment factories are, in fact, the shock troops of the global economy. Visit a country that has just recently opened itself up to foreign investment, and you will likely find a host of garment factories, even if there are very few other multinational enterprises located there. Nicaragua and Cambodia are typical examples—poor, war-torn countries that have attracted scores of garment manufacturers but very little else in the way of foreign investment. Low tech, intensely dependent on cheap labor, clothing manufacturing is the crest of the corporate globalization wave.

Separate forces meet in a shameful mix: A footloose industry scours the world for the cheapest wages; countries eager for any kind of investment auction off their workers to the lowest bidder; government regulators deliberately look the other way when abuses occur in order to keep foreign investors happy. It's that combination of desperate profit-seeking and equally desperate investment pursuit which has created the race to the bottom that is at the root of the sweatshop resurgence.

For workers, the current system is a trap. The apparel manufacturers fear that if they raise their workers' wages, and therefore their prices to the US retailers, the US retailers will simply go someplace with even cheaper workers. The threat is real. Because the garment industry is so mobile, and because the purchasing ability of the retailers is so flexible—they can shift sourcing from one country to another in a matter of a fashion season—any country that raises its wages or enforces its workers' rights risks, as mainstream economists say, "pricing itself out of the market." That risk is what keeps wages low as long as the retail corporations demand the cheapest price possible.

The race to the bottom is happening. Regardless of which country they live in, garment workers endure the same long hours, the same hard work in demeaning environments, and same small wages.

How Do Free Trade Agreements Contribute to Sweatshop Abuses?

So-called "free trade" agreements such as NAFTA [North American Free Trade Agreement] have exacerbated this race to the bottom. NAFTA is, in a sense, an "investors' rights" treaty. That is, it gives investors new abilities to move production facilities and finished goods and services across international borders while providing investors with guarantees that governments won't get in the way of their business.

Lower tariff rates and the elimination of import quotas make it easier for goods and services to move across borders. At the same time, NAFTA's rules have given corporations assurances that government regulations won't interfere with their operations. NAFTA gave corporations new legal rights to sue national governments for the enactment of policies that can undermine their profits.

The changes wrought by NAFTA gave US and Canadian corporations new incentives to relocate factories to Mexico, where wages are lower and labor unions weaker. This contributed to an increase in the number of sweatshops in Mexico.

Corporations will gain more powers to act without being accountable to their workers, the communities in which they operate, or the public in general.

Corporations have been happy to use the new advantages given them by "free trade" agreements, especially when facing organized workforces in the wealthier countries. According to a study conducted under the auspices of NAFTA's labor side agreement, 90 percent of 400 plant closings or threatened plant closings in the US in a five-year period occurred illegally in the face of a union-organizing drive.

If the FTAA becomes reality, the race to the bottom will accelerate as corporations gain even more ability to move throughout the Western Hemisphere. This will spread sweatshop-style production to new places, while making current sweatshops even more miserable as workers are asked to toil for less and less. Under the FTAA, corporations will be able to pit exploited workers in Mexico against even more desperate workers in countries such as Haiti.

In fact, this dismal prospect is already becoming reality. China's entry into the World Trade Organization has led to some companies moving their factories from Mexico to China, where wages are cheaper. Since 2000, about 350 [maquiladoras] have left Mexico in search of cheaper labor and looser environmental regulations. Approximately 300 of these have moved to China.

Under the FTAA, the corporations will gain more powers to act without being accountable to their workers, the communities in which they operate, or the public in general. The corporations' gain will come at workers' expense, as more and more people can find only jobs that offer no dignity and provide no opportunity. The FTAA will be a boon for the sweatshop economy.

9

Free Trade Agreements and Globalization Benefit Workers

Daniel Griswold

Daniel Griswold is the director of the Center for Trade Policy Studies at the Cato Institute, a nonprofit, public policy research foundation that advocates for the principles of limited government, free markets, and individual liberty.

Free trade and a globalized economy are raising labor standards in the United States as well as in developing countries. According to the Federal Reserve Board, America's factories produced 50 percent more in 2006 after enacting the North American Free Trade Agreement (NAFTA) than in the early 1990s. And millions of people in developing countries are rising out of poverty and dreadful working conditions because of increased global trade. In fact, the International Labor Organization recently reported a drop in child labor, with more children attending school. If Americans truly seek higher labor standards worldwide, they should support and encourage free trade; demanding trade sanctions would only hurt the people who need the most help.

Expanding trade with developing countries not only promotes more U.S. exports, but just as importantly it provides a wider array of affordable products for American consumers—such as shoes, clothing, toys, and sporting goods.

Daniel Griswold, "The Best 'Anti-Sweatshop' Policy: Expanding U.S. Trade with Developing Countries," Testimony before the Trade, Tourism, and Economic Development Subcommittee of the U.S. Senate Commerce, Science, and Transportation Committee, Hearing on Overseas Sweatshop Abuses, Their Impact on U.S. Workers, and the Need for Anti-Sweatshop Legislation, February 14, 2007. Reproduced by permission. Not printed exactly as published; edits made.

Tens of millions of American families benefit from more vigorous price competition in goods that make our lives better every day at home and the office. Lower prices and more choices translate directly into higher real compensation and living standards for American workers.

Free Trade Does Not Undermine American Workers

American workers are not pitted in zero-sum competition with workers in poor countries. There is no global "race to the bottom" on labor standards. Through specialization, global incomes and working conditions can rise for workers in all countries that participate in the global economy. American workers can compete profitably in world markets because we are so much more productive. Because of our education, infrastructure, efficient domestic markets, the rule of law, political stability, and a generally open economy, American workers compete and prosper in a broad range of sectors. As our country has become more globalized in the past 25 years, American workers and their families have enjoyed significant increases in real incomes, compensation, and wealth.

Openness to trade and investment leads to faster growth, which leads to higher wages and labor standards.

Nor has trade with developing countries undermined America's manufacturing base. According to the latest figures from the Federal Reserve Board, the output of America's factories in 2006 was more than 50 percent higher than in the early 1990s before NAFTA [North American Free Trade Agreement] and the World Trade Organization came into being. American factories are producing more aircraft and pharmaceuticals, more sophisticated machinery and semiconductors, more chemicals and even more passenger vehicles and parts than 15 years ago. It is true that output of clothing, shoes, and other low-tech goods has been declining, but those are not the industries of the future for the world's most sophisticated economy. U.S. factories can produce more with fewer workers because manufacturing productivity has been growing so rapidly.

If there were a "race to the bottom," then the lower wages and labor standards in less developed countries should be attracting large shares of global investment. Of course, developing countries attract foreign investment in those sectors in which they enjoy a comparative advantage, such as light manufacturing, but in fact, the large majority of manufacturing foreign direct investment (FDI) flows between rich countries. When U.S. multinational companies look to invest abroad, their primary motivation is not a search for low wages and low standards. Far more important than lower costs are access to wealthy consumers, a skilled workforce, modern infrastructure, rule of law, political stability, and freedom to trade and repatriate profits. That is why most outward U.S. FDI flows to other high-income, high-standard countries. Between 2003 and 2005, more than 80 percent of U.S. direct manufacturing abroad flowed to the European Union, Canada, Japan, South Korea, Taiwan, and Singapore.

Free Trade Agreements Improve Pay and Working Conditions

Openness to trade and investment leads to faster growth, which leads to higher wages and labor standards, including so-called core worker rights. That is why the world's most developed economies, which account for most of the world's trade and attract most of its foreign direct investment, also pay the highest wages, and maintain the highest labor standards related to freedom of association, discrimination, forced labor, and child labor.

Trade and globalization are lifting wages and working conditions for hundreds of millions of people in developing countries. The pay and conditions offered in foreign-owned factories are almost always far higher than those offered in the domestic economy. In fact, working for multinational companies that export are almost invariably the best jobs available in poor countries. Those jobs offer poor workers, especially young women, their best opportunity at financial independence and the simple pleasures and dignities of life we take for granted.

For example, apparel jobs are among the lowest-paying manufacturing jobs in our country, but they are among the best paying in poor countries. A recent study from San Jose University found that the apparel industry actually pays its foreign workers well enough for them to rise above the poverty line in the countries where they invest. In Honduras, for example, where college protestors have targeted its alleged "sweatshops," the average apparel worker earns $13 per day, compared to the $2 a day or less earned by 44 percent of the country's population.

By raising incomes in poor countries, free trade and globalization have helped to pull millions of kids out of the workforce and put them in school where they belong.

Rising levels of global trade have lifted hundreds of millions of people out of the worst kind of poverty and working conditions. According to the World Bank, the share of the world's population living in absolute poverty, defined as an income equivalent to one U.S. dollar per day or less, has been cut in half since 1981, from 40.4 percent to 19.4 percent. Poverty has fallen the most rapidly in those areas of the world that have globalized the most rapidly, especially China. It has fallen the least or actually increased in those regions that are the least touched by globalization, in particular sub-Saharan Africa.

Globalization Reduces Child Labor

Openness to trade and the growth it brings exert a positive impact on the welfare of children in less developed countries by reducing rates of child labor. The International Labor Organization recently reported that the number of children in the workforce rather than in school worldwide has dropped by 11 percent since its last report in 2002, to about 200 million. The number working in the most hazardous jobs has dropped even more steeply, by 26 percent.

Globalization is a major reason for the positive trend in child labor. As household incomes rise in developing countries, especially wages paid to adult females, fewer families face the economic necessity of sending their children to work. Studies confirm that labor force participation rates by children ages 10 to 14 decline significantly with rising GNP [gross national product] per capita.

The overwhelming majority of child laborers toiling in poor countries work in sectors far removed from the global economy. More than 80 percent work without pay, usually for their parents or other family members and typically in subsistence farming. Most other child laborers work for small-scale domestic enterprises, typically non-traded services such as shoe shining, newspaper delivery, and domestic service. A report by the U.S. Department of Labor found, "Only a very small percentage of all child workers, probably less than five percent, are employed in export industries in manufacturing and mining. And they are not commonly found in large enterprises; but rather in small and medium-sized firms and in neighborhood and home settings."

Globalization is not the cause of bad working conditions but the best hope for improving them.

Parents in poor countries do not love their children any less than we love our own. When they succeed in rising above a subsistence income, the first thing they typically do is remove their children from working on the farm, domestic service, or factory and enroll them in school. By raising incomes in poor countries, free trade and globalization have helped to pull millions of kids out of the workforce and put them in school where they belong.

In Central America, trade liberalization and other reforms of the past two decades have spurred not only growth in incomes but also measurable social progress. According to the World Bank, literacy rates for men and women 15 and older have risen significantly in every one of the six DR-CAFTA [Dominican Republic-Central America Free Trade Agreement] countries since 1980. In fact, between 1980 and 2001, the average literacy rate in the region has increased from 67 percent to above 80 percent. At the same time, the percentage of children ages 10 to 14 who are in the workforce has been steadily declining in all six countries. The average share of children in the labor force across the six countries has dropped from 17.4 percent in 1980 to 10.0 percent in 2002. Expanding trade with the United States will likely accelerate those positive trends.

It is certainly true that working conditions in less developed countries can strike Western observers as unacceptable if not appalling. But two points need to be considered. First, wages and working conditions are likely to be even worse in non-trade-oriented sectors, such as services and subsistence agriculture, sectors that have been largely untouched by globalization. Second, poor working conditions in those countries are not a new development but have always been a chronic fact of life. "Sweatshop" conditions persist today not because of globalization, a relatively new phenomenon, but because of previous decades of protectionism, inflation, economic mismanagement, hostility to foreign investment, and a lack of legally defined property rights. Globalization is not the cause of bad working conditions but the best hope for improving them.

Trade Sanctions Impair Poor Countries

Perversely, withholding trade benefits because of allegedly low standards would in effect punish those countries for being poor. It would deprive them of the expanded market access that offers the best hope to raise incomes and standards. The use of trade sanctions would target the very export industries that typically pay the highest wages and maintain [the] highest standards in those countries.

The effect of sanctions would be to shrink the more globally integrated sectors that are pulling standards upwards, forcing workers into informal, domestic sectors where wages, working conditions, and labor-rights protections are much lower. Lower wages paid to parents would make it more difficult for families on marginal incomes to keep children in school and out of fields or factories. "Tough" sanctions to allegedly enforce higher standards would be tough only on the poorest people in the world.

Demanding that poor countries eliminate child labor under threat of trade sanctions can easily backfire. In 1993, Congress seemed poised to pass the U.S. Child Labor Deterrence Act, which would have banned imports of textiles made by child workers. Anticipating its passage, the Bangladeshi textile industry dismissed 50,000 children from factories. Most of those children did not end up in school but instead fell into prostitution and other "occupations" far more degrading than weaving cloth in a factory.

America's trade policy is already biased against workers in poor countries without making it more so through "anti-sweatshop" legislation. The United States and other rich countries currently impose their highest trade barriers against products of [the] most importance to poor countries: clothing, textiles, and agricultural products. In fact, our average tariff imposed on imports from poor countries is about four times higher than those imposed on imports from other rich countries. Our regressive tariff system imposes punitive tariffs on workers in some of the poorest countries in the world. According to the Progressive Policy Institute, the U.S. government collects more tariff revenue on the $2 billion in mostly hats and T-shirts we import from Bangladesh in a year than on the $30 billion in planes, computers, medicines, and wine we import from France. Imports from Cambodia face an average tariff of 16 [percent], ten times higher than the average 1.6 percent we impose on all imports.

If members of Congress want to encourage higher labor standards abroad, they should support policies that encourage free trade and investment flows so that less developed nations can grow more rapidly.

The Best Policy at Home and Abroad

Our trade policies also hurt the world's poorest farmers and their children. A 2002 study for the National Bureau of Economic Research found that higher rice prices in Vietnam were associated with significant declines in child labor rates. Specifically, a 30 percent increase in rice prices accounted for a decrease of children in the workforce of 1 million, or 9 percent. The drop was most pronounced among girls ages 14 and 15. As the incomes of rice-growing families rose, they chose to use their additional resources to remove their children from work in the field and send them to school. If U.S. rice subsidies are indeed depressing global rice prices, as evidence confirms, then those same programs are plausibly responsible for keeping tens of thousands of young girls in Vietnam and other poor countries in the labor force rather than school.

Attempts to "enforce" labor and environmental standards through trade sanctions are not only unnecessary but also counterproductive. Sanctions deprive poor countries of the international trade and investment opportunities they need to raise overall living standards. Sanctions tend to strike at the very export industries in less developed countries that typically pay the highest wages and follow the highest standards, forcing production and employment into less-globalized sectors, where wages and standards are almost always lower. The end result of sanctions is the very opposite of what their advocates claim to seek.

If members of Congress want to encourage higher labor standards abroad, they should support policies that encourage free trade and investment flows so that less developed nations can grow more rapidly. As a complementary policy, Congress could seek a more robust International Labor Organization that could systematically monitor and report on enforcement of labor rights in member countries. Meanwhile, civil society organizations are free to raise public awareness through campaigns and boycotts, while importers can cater to consumer preferences for higher standards through labeling and other promotions.

The demand for trade sanctions as a tool to enforce labor standards confronts Americans with a false choice. In reality, the best policy for promoting economic growth at home and abroad—an economy open to global trade and investment—is also the best policy for promoting higher labor standards.

10

Governments Should Not Boycott Sweatshop Products

Cheryl Grey

Cheryl Grey is a contributing writer to the online magazine Citizen Economists *and writes a blog regarding current economic subjects.*

To many Americans, sweatshops seem horrific, with back-breaking hours and unhealthy working conditions—so much so that the honorable reaction ought to be a boycott of sweatshop products. In reality, however, boycotting such products would deprive workers the opportunity to rise above poverty, and deprive countries the opportunity to' develop effective economies. Although it is not a pretty picture, the sweatshop system has proved to be successful—Japan's current economy is an example—and should be allowed to run its course.

Even in our modern world, sweatshops remain a horrifying reality, with hundreds of thousands of the world's poor and defenseless people exploited by wealthy factory owners and greedy supervisors. Their jobs, perhaps better termed slavery, involve back-breaking hours in pitiful conditions, sometimes using toxic chemicals without adequate ventilation or protective gloves or goggles, for pennies per day. Stories of children stitching fancy beadwork by candlelight at midnight, female workers forced to provide sexual favors to keep their jobs and workers refusing to drink fluids in sweltering heat to prevent the necessity of bathroom breaks are all too common and all too true.

Cheryl Grey, "Outsourcing: The Good Side of Asian Sweatshops," *Citizen Economists*, August 14, 2008. Reproduced by permission of the author.

So, how could there be a good side to this? And why would any self-respecting industrialized nation purchase products made in such a fashion? The instinctive, gut-level reaction is to boycott these goods; is that wrong?

In a word, yes.

Boycotting goods made by sweatshop labor only hurts the workers.

Better than the Alternative

On average, the employees of sweatshops work there because they have no better alternative. Children work in such conditions, not instead of going to school but because they have no school to attend or no means to support themselves if they do. Parents work there because the alternative is watching their children drop out of school and work . . . or starve.

It's a painful fact that boycotting goods made by sweatshop labor only hurts the workers, not the factory owners. In 1993, a U.S. boycott forced Bangladeshi factories to quit utilizing child labor. According to Oxfam [a group of nongovernmental organizations working to fight poverty and injustice], most of those displaced children were forced into worse positions, including prostitution—when their first choice had been to sew clothing for Wal-Mart shoppers.

Being without better alternatives, the people who have sweatshop jobs are often glad to have them and see them as a positive beginning for a better life. [Journalists] Nicholas D. Kristof and Sheryl WuDunn, who won the Pulitzer Prize in 1991 for their coverage of China's Tiananmen Square massacre [involving a 1989 student protest], recounted multiple stories of Chinese sweatshop workers who were puzzled when Western journalists bemoaned their twelve-hour-plus workdays, seven days per week. More than one young woman they interviewed said how great it was that the factory allowed them to work such long hours, and others commented they had taken that job deliberately over others in the area to earn more hourly pay.

Since that interview in 1987, more companies invested in the area and additional factories opened across southern China. Although this workers' state could still use a few stout labor unions, workers are now more mobile, wages have more than quintupled and conditions have improved as factories compete for the best workers. More people now work for private industry than for the state (although it's also true that unemployment has risen as a result). Although the yuan's [Chinese currency] exchange rate is still controlled by the government, its purchasing power has risen to approximately one-sixteenth that of the U.S. dollar. The rivers of bicycles once common in Chinese cities are being replaced by cars and even SUVs [sport utility vehicles], with gasoline subsidized by the government.

Opportunity for Betterment

According to an article by [entrepreneur and chief executive officer of the nonprofit Flow] Michael Strong in 2006, roughly 1.2 million people rise above poverty in China every month by moving to an urban area and taking a job that pays less than US$2 per day. He claims that Wal-Mart, through allowing developing economies access to industrialized markets, has helped more of the world's desperately poor than the World Bank and relates the story of a Mongolian student who, when he heard U.S. college students ripping into sweatshops, shouted out, "Please, give us your sweatshops!"

Strong also points out, quite correctly, that a line must be drawn between criminal exploitation and market economics. Workers deserve decent wages and working conditions that won't kill them, not only in developed nations but also in the backwoods of beyond. But to achieve that requires not fewer sweatshops but more of them, clustered together to create competition for workers in the Chinese pattern.

If China continues growing at its current rate, in 2031 it will reach a standard of living comparable to that in the U.S. It's the same path taken by Japan in the 1950s and 1960s and the Asian tigers [Hong Kong, Singapore, South Korea, and Taiwan] in the 1970s and 1980s.

It's an ugly path, dirty and brutal. But it's proven to work. Can the same be said for other forms of foreign aid?

11

Unions Promote Anti-Sweatshop Movement to Further Their Own Agenda

Thomas J. DiLorenzo

Thomas J. DiLorenzo is a professor of economics at Loyola College in Maryland and a senior faculty member at the think tank Ludwig von Mises Institute.

In order to survive, American labor unions believe they must prohibit the spread of capitalism to third world countries because of the competition from nonunion labor that would result. Capitalism—the economic system that is based primarily on competition of prices and production in a free market—has been proved to increase jobs and raise wages, and by extension to bring economic stability and prosperity to countries. Yet despite such benefits, members of American labor unions, who show no regard for the well-being of anyone but themselves, discourage foreign investment in third world countries.

One of the oldest myths about capitalism is the notion that factories that offer the poor higher wages to lure them off the streets (and away from lives of begging, stealing, prostitution, or worse) or away from back-breaking farm labor somehow impoverishes and exploits them. They are said to work in "sweatshops" for "subsistence wages." That was the claim made by socialists and unionists in the early days of the industrial revolution, and it is still made today by the same category of malcontents—usually by people who have never themselves performed manual labor and experienced breaking a sweat while working. (I am not referring here to the red herring claim that most foreign "sweatshops" utilize some kind of slave labor. This is an outrageous propaganda ploy designed to portray defenders of free markets as being in favor of slavery.)

If the labor unions have their way, the poor whose lives are improved by their employment by multinational corporations would all be thrown out of work.

Discouraging Competition

The self-interest of labor unions in this anti-capitalist crusade has always been transparent: Unions cannot exist without somehow prohibiting competition from non-union labor, whether that labor is at home or abroad. Thus, they wage campaigns of propaganda, intimidation, or violence against non-union workers, whether they are in Indiana or Indonesia. They are not in the least concerned about the well-being of the Third World poor. If the labor unions have their way, the poor whose lives are improved by their employment by multinational corporations would all be thrown out of work, many of whom would be forced to resort to crime, prostitution, or starvation. *That* is the "moral high ground" that has been staked out on college campuses all over America, where unions have been successful in instigating "anti-sweatshop" campaigns, seminars, and protests.

That the anti-factory movement has always been motivated by either the socialists' desire to destroy industrial civilization, or by the inherently non-competitive nature of organized labor, is further evidenced by the fact that there was never an "anti-sweat-farm movement." Farm labor is still as rigorous as any physical labor, as it was 150 years ago. Indeed, in the early days of the industrial revolution—and in Third

World countries today—one reason ... families had so many more children than they do in wealthier countries today is that they were viewed as potential farm hands. [Former U.S. president] Abraham Lincoln had less than one year of formal education because his parents, like most others on the early nineteenth-century American frontier, needed him as a farm hand. But since agriculture was not considered to be a form of capitalism, and did not pose any real threat to unionized labor, there was never any significant social protest over it.

Discouraging the Benefits of Capitalism

In a forthcoming [2006] article in the *Journal of Labor Research* [economists] Ben Powell and David Skarbek present the results of a survey of "sweatshops" in eleven Third World countries. In nine of the eleven countries, "sweatshop" wages in foreign factories located there were higher than the average. In Honduras, where almost half the working population lives on $2/day, "sweatshops" pay $13.10/day. "Sweatshop" wages are more than double the national average in Cambodia, Haiti, Nicaragua, and Honduras. The implication of this for all those naïve college students (and faculty) who have been duped into becoming anti-sweatshop protesters is that they should support and encourage *more* direct foreign investment in the Third World if they are at all concerned about the economic well-being of the people there.

It is never the workers in countries like Honduras who protest the existence of a new factory there built by a Nike or a General Motors. The people there benefit as consumers as well as workers, [because] there are more (and cheaper) consumer goods manufactured and sold in their country (as well as in other parts of the world). Capital investment of this sort is infinitely superior to the alternative—foreign aid—which always empowers the governmental recipients of the "aid," making things even worse for the private economies of "aid" recipients. Market-based capital investment is always far superior to politicized capital allocation. Moreover, if the foreign investment fails, the economic burden falls on the investors and stockholders, not the poor Third World country. . . .

Perhaps one of the strongest virtues of foreign "sweat-shops" is that they weaken the hand of American labor unions.

Another virtue of foreign investment in the Third World is that it has the potential of transferring such knowledge to countries where it previously did not exist—or at least was not very prevalent. It is not only technology that the poor countries need, but the culture of capitalism. Without it they will never dig their way out of poverty.

Discouraging the Potential for Economic Prosperity

The existence of foreign factories in poor countries also creates what economists call "agglomeration economies." The location of a factory will cause many businesses of all types to sprout all around the factory to serve the factory itself as well as all of the employees. Thus, it is not just the factory jobs that are created. Furthermore, a successful investment in a poor country will send a signal to other potential investors that there is a stable environment for investment there, which can lead to even more investment, job creation, and prosperity.

Capital investment in poor countries will cause wages to rise over time by increasing the marginal productivity of labor. This is what has occurred since the dawn of the industrial revolution and it is occurring today all around the world. Discouraging such investment, which is the objective of the anti-sweatshop movement, will do the opposite and cause wages to stagnate.

Finally, perhaps one of the strongest virtues of foreign "sweatshops" is that they weaken the hand of American labor unions. With few exceptions, American unions have long been at the forefront of anti-capitalist ideology and have supported virtually all the destructive tax and regulatory policies that have been so poisonous to American capitalism. Unions believe that they cannot exist unless workers can be convinced that employers are the enemies of the working class, if not society, and that they (the workers) need unions to protect them from these exploiters.

If you want to support the Third World poor, purchase *more* of the products that they labor to make in the capitalist enterprises that have located there.

12

Sweatshop Inspections Are Important

T.A. Frank

T.A. Frank is a consulting editor of the Washington Monthly, *a politically independent magazine that covers issues about government and politics in America. Frank is also an Irvine Fellow at the New America Foundation, a nonprofit public policy institute and think tank located in Washington, D.C.*

Operating under the belief that getting the most out of workers results in earning the highest profits, some companies violate labor laws by physically abusing workers, enforcing excessive overtime work, and paying insufficient wages. As a result, factories (whether in the United States or foreign countries) need to be consistently monitored to ensure ethical and humane labor standards are being followed. Despite the fact that some companies have learned how to lie and cheat to circumvent the inspections (such as falsifying time cards or intimidating workers), monitoring factories to enforce labor laws is important and can produce positive change in the long run.

I remember one particularly bad factory in China. It produced outdoor tables, parasols, and gazebos, and the place was a mess. Work floors were so crowded with production materials that I could barely make my way from one end to the other. In one area, where metals were being chemically treated, workers squatted at the edge of steaming pools as if contemplating a sudden, final swim. The dormitories were filthy: the hallways were strewn with garbage—orange peels, tea leaves—and the only way for anyone to bathe was to fill a bucket with cold water. In a country where workers normally suppress their complaints for fear of getting fired, employees at this factory couldn't resist telling us the truth. "We work so hard for so little pay," said one middle-aged woman with undisguised anger. We could only guess how hard—the place kept no time cards. Painted in large characters on the factory walls was a slogan: "If you don't work hard today, look hard for work tomorrow." Inspirational, in a way.

Private monitoring, if done properly, can do a lot of good.

"Corporate Social Responsibility Monitoring"

I was there because, six years ago [in 2002], I had a job at a Los Angeles firm that specialized in the field of "compliance consulting," or "corporate social responsibility monitoring." It's a service that emerged in the mid-1990s after the press started to report on bad factories around the world and companies grew concerned about protecting their reputations. With an increase of protectionist sentiment in the United States, companies that relied on cheap labor abroad were feeling vulnerable to negative publicity. They still are.

Today [2008], labor standards are once again in the news. [U.S. presidential candidates] Barack Obama and Hillary Clinton have criticized trade deals such as NAFTA [North American Free Trade Agreement] as unfair to American workers, and the new thinking is that trade agreements should include strict labor standards. Obama has cited a recent free trade agreement with Peru as an example of how to go forward. I hope he's right, but let's remember that NAFTA was also hailed, in its day, for including labor protections. Our solutions on paper have proved hard to enforce. Peru attempts to remedy some of the problems of NAFTA, but we're still advancing slowly in the dark.

In the meantime, as governments contemplate such matters on a theoretical level, what's happening on the ground is mostly in the hands of the private sector. Companies police themselves, often using hired outside help. That was the specialty of my company. Visit the Web site of almost any large American retailer or apparel manufacturer and you're likely to see a section devoted to "ethical sourcing" or "our compliance program." (Those are terms for making sure that your suppliers aren't using factories that will land you on the front page of the *New York Times*.) Read on and you'll often see that the company boasts of having a code of conduct that its suppliers must follow—a code of labor standards by which the factories in question will be regularly measured and monitored. Are they to be believed? Well, yes and no. Private monitoring, if done properly, can do a lot of good. But it's a tricky thing.

Investigating Terrible Labor Conditions

A simplified story of Nike may be the best way to introduce the origins of the type of work I was in. In the 1960s, Nike (before it was named Nike) based its business on the premise that the company would not manufacture shoes—it would only design and market them. The physical goods would be produced by independent contractors in countries such as Japan or Taiwan, where labor was, at the time, cheap. In short, Nike would be offices, not factories. The idea was innovative and hugely profitable, and countless companies producing everything from sweaters to toys to exercise equipment have since adopted it. It is now standard.

The problem that arose for Nike and many other companies, however, was that the media, starting in the 1990s, began to run stories on terrible labor conditions in factories in Asia. When consumers started to get angry, Nike and many other companies were nonplussed. We're just buying these shoes, they said—it's not our business how Mr. X runs his factory. And they had a point. If, for example, I learned that my dry cleaner was paying his employees less than minimum wage, I might feel bad about it, but I doubt I'd spend hours vetting alternative dry cleaners for labor compliance. I've got too much else to worry about in life, including my shirts. But such musings hardly make for a great press release, and Nike's case included nasty allegations about child labor—twelve-year-old Americans playing with soccer balls sewn by twelve-year-old Pakistanis, that sort of thing. The company's stock value sank.

In this same period, the U.S. Department of Labor, led by Robert Reich, began cracking down on sweatshops within the United States and publicizing the names of firms who were their customers. Because of this, companies such as mine began to offer their services as independent, for-profit monitors of factory labor conditions. We would act as early-warning systems against shady suppliers who mistreated their workers. Based on the reports we provided, our clients could choose either to sever their relations with a given supplier or to pressure them to improve. Business at my old company is still going strong.

In Los Angeles, where small garment shops of, say, thirty employees were the main focus, we usually worked in pairs and did three inspections a day. Outside the country, where the factories were often quite large (several thousand employees) and made anything from toys to gym equipment, we worked alone or in pairs and did one or two a day. The procedures were similar, but the inspections were more thorough abroad. While one of us might tour the work floors to note all the health and safety violations (the gazebo factory, for instance, had no secondary exits, no guarding on machines, no first aid supplies, no eye protection—the list kept going), the other might review permits, employee files, and payroll records to see what shortcomings were apparent on paper alone.

A collection of crisp time cards that showed every employee arriving within seconds of the next was easy to spot as having been punched by a single worker standing alone at the time clock.

Then we would begin interviewing employees in private, usually twenty or so, hoping to learn from them what our eyes wouldn't tell us. Did the factory confiscate personal documents, such as identity cards, and use them as ransom? (This was most common in the [Persian Gulf States, which include Kuwait and Qatar], where foreign laborers from places like Bangladesh could find themselves effectively enslaved. But bosses sometimes confiscated national identification documents in China, too.) Were employees free to enter and leave the compound? How many hours a week did they *really* work—regardless of what the time cards might say?

Getting Bamboozled

Unfortunately, we missed stuff. All inspections do. And sometimes it was embarrassing. At one follow-up inspection of a factory in Bangkok at which I'd noted some serious but common wage violations, the auditors who followed me found pregnant employees hiding on the roof and Burmese import workers earning criminally low wages. Whoops. On the other hand, sometimes I was the one who uncovered what others had missed. A lot of it had to do with luck. Was the right document visible on the work floor? Did we choose the right employees for interviews—the ones who were willing to confide in outsiders? If we were working through a translator, was his manner of speaking to people soothing?

The major challenge of inspections was simply staying ahead of the factories we monitored. False time cards and payroll records, whole days spent coaching employees on how to lie during interviews, and even renaming certain factory buildings in order to create a smaller Potemkin village [a facade designed to hide undesirable conditions]—all of these were techniques used by contractors to try to fool us. We were able to detect some of them. A collection of crisp time cards that showed every employee arriving within seconds of the next was easy to spot as having been punched by a single worker standing alone at the time clock. An employee whose recollection of hours worked differed markedly from her time sheet was another indication of shady bookkeeping. . . .

Because any inspection misses something, there were factories that managed to embarrass everyone. In 2000, *Business-Week* published an expose about a factory in Guangdong, China, the Chun Si Enterprise Handbag Factory, which made bags for Wal-Mart. Titled "Inside a Chinese Sweatshop: 'A Life of Fines and Beating,'" the article described a nightmarish place in which nine hundred workers were locked in a walled compound all day, and security guards "regularly punched and hit workers for talking back to managers or even for walking too fast." The reporting, by Dexter Roberts and Aaron Bernstein, was superb. Unfortunately, that reporting led to the door of my company, which had been among the auditors monitoring the factory for Wal-Mart. While they had found excessive overtime work and insufficient pay, inspectors had missed the captive workers and physical abuse.

When companies make a genuine effort, the results can be impressive: safe factories that pay legal wages.

To be sure, the Chun Si Enterprise Handbag Factory episode was a debacle. (I have no inside account of the story, since it took place several years before my arrival.) I suspect, however, that the fault lay with Wal-Mart as much as with the inspectors. I say this because there's a broader point here: Monitoring by itself is meaningless. It [works only] when the company that's commissioning it has a sincere interest in improving the situation. In the case of Chun Si, inspectors visited five times, according to *BusinessWeek*, and kept finding trouble. Now, anyone in the business knows that when inspections uncover safety violations or wage underpayment more than once or twice—let alone five times—it's a sign that bigger problems are lurking beneath. Companies rarely get bamboozled about this sort of thing unless they want to.

And many prefer to be bamboozled, because it's cheaper. While companies like to boast of having an ethical sourcing program, such programs make it harder to hire the lowest bidder. Because many companies still want to hire the lowest bidder, "ethical sourcing" often becomes a game. The simplest way to play it is by placing an order with a cheap supplier and ending the relationship once the goods have been delivered. In the meantime, inspectors get sent to evaluate the factory— perhaps several times, [as] they keep finding problems—until the client, seeing no improvement in the labor conditions, severs the bond and moves on to the next low-priced, equally suspect supplier. . . .

Producing Positive Change

While private monitoring can be misused, however, when it's done right it can really produce positive change. I've seen it. When companies make a genuine effort, the results can be impressive: safe factories that pay legal wages. That sounds modest, but it's actually hard to achieve in any country. Just visit a garment shop in Los Angeles.

At my company, I quickly figured out which clients cared. The first test was whether they conducted "pre-sourcing"— inspections of labor conditions before placing an order instead of after. This small step truly separates the top-rung companies from the pack, because to prescreen is to forgo the temptation of hiring the cheapest suppliers. (Those suppliers are the cheapest because they tend to break the rules, so they usually fail the preliminary inspection.) The second test was whether the company had a long-term relationship with its suppliers. Long-term commitments are what motivate both parties to behave: the supplier wants to preserve the relationship, and the customer wants to preserve its reputation. The third test was whether the company requested unannounced inspections as opposed to ones that were arranged in advance. The advantages of this are self-evident. And the final test was whether the company made inspection results public. This was almost never done. . . .

When a Chinese factory saves money by making its employees breathe hazardous fumes . . . that's wrong.

As for those who feel especially strongly about the issue and kick up a (peaceful) fuss about sweatshops, I think they're doing a valuable thing. Even when they take actions that are sometimes off-base—such as continuing to boycott Nike when its competitors are the bigger problem—the effect is still, overall, good: it scares businesses into taking compliance more seriously. Boycotts, protests, letters to Congress, saber-rattling lawmakers, media exposes—they do have an impact. And just imagine if members of Congress or the executive branch made an effort to praise or shame companies for their records with foreign suppliers and to encourage transparent monitoring in the private sector. I suspect it would do more for international labor standards in months than the most intricate trade agreements could do in years.

I don't pretend that everything monitoring brings about is for the best. An example: Mattel's factories in China are superb, but workers there often earn less than their peers in shadier factories because their employers confine them to shorter workweeks to avoid paying overtime. Another: You may rightly hate the idea of child labor, but firing a fourteen-year-old in Indonesia from a factory job because she is fourteen does nothing but deprive her of income she is understandably desperate to keep. (She'll find worse work elsewhere, most likely, or simply go hungry.) A third: Small village factories may break the rules, but they often operate in a humane and basically sensible way, and I didn't enjoy lecturing their owners about the necessity of American-style time cards and fifteen-minute breaks. But labor standards anywhere have a tendency to create such problems. They're enacted in the hope that the good outweighs the bad.

One final thought: If you're like me, part of you feels that Peru's labor standards are basically Peru's business. It's our job to worry about standards here at home. But that sort of thinking doesn't work well in an era of globalization. We are, like it or not, profoundly affected by the labor standards of our trading partners. If their standards are low, they exert a downward pressure on our own. That's why monitoring and enforcement have such an important role to play. We don't expect developing nations to match us in what their workers earn. (A few dollars a day is a fortune in many nations.) But when a Chinese factory saves money by making its employees breathe hazardous fumes and, by doing so, closes down a U.S. factory that spends money on proper ventilation and masks, that's wrong. It's wrong by any measure. And that's what we can do something about if we try. It's the challenge we face as the walls come down, the dolls, pajamas, and televisions come in, and, increasingly, the future of our workers here is tied to that of workers who are oceans away.

Organizations to Contact

The editors have compiled the following list of organizations concerned with the issues debated in this book. The descriptions are derived from materials provided by the organizations. All have publications or information available for interested readers. The list was compiled on the date of publication of the present volume; the information provided here may change. Readers need to remember that many organizations take several weeks or longer to respond to inquiries.

Child Labor Coalition (CLC)
1701 K Street NW, Suite 1200, Washington, DC 20006
(202) 835-3323 • fax: (202) 835-0747
E-mail: childlabor@nclnet.org
Web site: www.stopchildlabor.org

The CLC, a group of more than twenty organizations, represents consumers, labor unions, educators, human rights and labor rights groups, child advocacy groups, and religious and women's groups. It was established in 1989 and is cochaired by the National Consumers League and the American Federation of Teachers. Its mission is to protect working youth and to promote legislation, programs, and initiatives to end child labor exploitation in the United States and abroad. The CLC's Web site offers news reports, press releases, and fact sheets, including "Children in the Fields: The Inequitable Treatment of Child Farmworkers" and "Youth Peddling Crews: Sweatshops of the Streets."

Children's Rights Information Network (CRIN)
East Studio, 2 Pontypool Place, London SE1 8QF
  United Kingdom
+44-20-7401-2257
E-mail: info@crin.org
Web site: www.crin.org

CRIN is an international network of children's rights organizations that supports the effective exchange of information about children and their rights to help implement the United Nations Convention on the Rights of the Child. The network publishes information on children's rights, including "Children and Adolescents Statement: Strategies for International Cooperation" and "Haiti: Lost Childhoods in Haiti."

Committee on the Rights of the Child (CRC)
Office of the United Nations High Commissioner
for Human Rights
Palais des Nations, Geneva 10   CH-1211
   Switzerland
+41 22-928-92-24 • fax: +41 22-928-90-10
Web site: www2.ohchr.org/english/bodies/crc

The CRC is a body of independent experts that monitors implementation of the United Nations Convention on the Rights of the Child by governments that have ratified the convention. The committee is made up of eighteen members from different countries who are considered to be experts in the field of human rights. The CRC publishes sessional and annual reports, press releases, and meeting summaries.

Corporate Watch
2958 24th Street, San Francisco, CA   94110
(510) 271-8050
Web site: www.corpwatch.org

Corporate Watch serves as an online magazine and resource center for investigating and analyzing corporate activity. Past articles have included "Jordan: An Ugly Side of Free Trade—Sweatshops," as well as news and action alerts. Its editors are committed to documenting the social, political, economic, and environmental misdeeds of corporations and to building support for human rights, environmental justice, and democratic control over corporations.

Human Rights Watch
350 Fifth Ave., New York, NY   10118-3299

(212) 290-4700 • fax: (212) 736-1300
E-mail: hrwnyc@hrw.org
Web site: www.hrw.org

Human Rights Watch is an activist organization dedicated to protecting the human rights of people around the world, including workers' rights. It investigates and exposes human rights violations and holds abusers accountable. It publishes an annual world report and, in its Children's Rights section, the organization has published "U.S.: Adopt Stronger Laws for Child Farmworkers" and "Indonesia: Protect Child Domestic Workers."

International Labor Organization (ILO)

4 Route des Morillons, Geneva 22   CH-1211
   Switzerland
+41 (0) 22-799-6111 • fax: +41 (0) 22-798-8685
E-mail: ilo@ilo.org
Web site: www.ilo.org

The ILO, a specialized agency of the United Nations, aims to advance opportunities for women and men to obtain decent and productive work in conditions of freedom, equity, security, and human dignity. Its main goals are to promote rights at work, encourage decent employment opportunities, enhance social protection, and strengthen dialogue in handling work-related issues. Among the ILO's numerous publications are newsletters; official reports, such as "World of Work Report: The Global Job Crisis"; and books, including *In Search of Decent Work—Migrant Workers' Rights: A Manual for Trade Unionists.*

National Consumers League (NCL)

1701 K Street NW, Suite 1200, Washington, DC   20006
(202) 835-3323 • fax: (202) 835-0747
E-mail: info@nclnet.org
Web site: www.nclnet.org

NCL works to protect and promote the economic and social interests of America's consumers through education, investigation, and research. Its members want to ensure that goods are produced under fair, safe, and healthy working conditions that foster quality products for consumers and a decent standard of living for workers. NCL worked for the first minimum wage laws, overtime compensation, and the child labor provisions in the Fair Labor Standards Act. The league publishes various articles on U.S. and international labor, including "Protecting Working Youth Should Be a Priority."

National Labor Committee (NLC)

5 Gateway Center, 6th Floor, Pittsburgh, PA   15222
(412) 562-2406 • fax: (412) 562-2411
E-mail: nlc@nlcnet.org
Web site: www.nlcnet.org

The committee seeks to educate and actively engage the U.S. public on human and labor rights abuses by corporations. Through education and activism, it works to end labor and human rights violations, ensure a living wage, and help workers and their families live and work with dignity. It produces videos, posters, and reports, including "Broken Lives: Behind U.S. Production in China" and "Child Labor Is Back."

Save the Children

54 Wilton Road, Westport, CT   06880
(800) 728-3843
Web site: www.savethechildren.org

Save the Children is an independent organization that seeks to ensure every child's right to survival, protection, education, and health. The organization publishes newsletters, research reports, issue briefs, fact sheets, and policy reports, including "Rewrite the Future: Education for Children in Conflict-Affected Countries."

United Nations Children's Fund (UNICEF)

UNICEF House, 3 United Nations Plaza, New York, NY   10017
(212) 686-5222 • fax: (212) 779-1679
E-mail: information@unicefusa.org
Web site: www.unicef.org

UNICEF, a nonpartisan organization, is mandated by the United Nations General Assembly to advocate for the protection of children's rights and to expand their opportunities. UNICEF upholds the Convention on the Rights of the Child and provides health care, clean water, improved nutrition, and education to millions of children worldwide. Among its publications are the yearly reports "The State of the World's Children," "Progress for Children," and an annual report, which spotlights significant results achieved on behalf of children around the world.

United Students Against Sweatshops (USAS)
1150 17th Street NW, Washington, DC   20036
(202) NO-SWEAT (667-9328)
E-mail: staff@usas.org
Web site: www.usas.org

USAS is a grassroots organization run entirely by youth and students. It advocates for just working conditions and long-term economic, social, and political empowerment for working people worldwide. The organization's Web site offers various news reports and posts, including "Details of the Historic Victory by Honduran Factory Workers."

Unite Here
275 Seventh Ave., New York, NY   10001-6708
(212) 265-7000
Web site: www.unitehere.org

Unite Here represents workers throughout the United States and Canada who work in the hospitality, gaming, food service, manufacturing, textile, laundry, and airport industries. The union fights for workers' rights in several industries. Its Web site includes updates on activists' accomplishments, news reports on labor legislation, and press releases.

Bibliography

Books

Priscilla Alderson   *Young Children's Rights: Exploring Beliefs, Principles and Practice*, 2nd Edition. Philadelphia: Jessica Kingsley Publishers, 2008.

David Bacon   *The Children of NAFTA: Labor Wars on the U.S./Mexico Border*. Berkeley: University of California Press, 2004.

Ishmael Beah   *A Long Way Gone: Memoirs of a Boy Soldier*. New York: Farrar, Straus and Giroux, 2007.

Raymond Bechard   *Unspeakable: The Hidden Truth Behind the World's Fastest Growing Crime*. New York: Compel Publishing, 2006.

Daniel E. Bender   *Sweated Work, Weak Bodies: Anti-Sweatshop Campaigns and Languages of Labor*. Piscataway, NJ: Rutgers University Press, 2004.

Rachel Burr   *Vietnam's Children in a Changing World*. Piscataway, NJ: Rutgers University Press, 2006.

Jill Esbenshade   *Monitoring Sweatshops: Workers, Consumers, and the Global Apparel Industry*. Philadelphia: Temple University Press, 2004.

Michael Freeman   *Children's Health and Children's Rights*. Boston: Martinus Nijhoff Publishers, 2006.

Jennifer Gordon   *Suburban Sweatshops: The Fight for Immigrant Rights*. Cambridge: Harvard University Press, 2005.

Wendy Herumin   *Child Labor Today: A Human Rights Issue*. Berkeley Heights, NJ: Enslow Publishers, 2008.

Hugh D. Hindman   *The World of Child Labor: An Historic and Regional Survey*. New York: Armonk, 2009.

Gilbert King   *Woman, Child for Sale: The New Slave Trade in the 21st Century*. New York: Chamberlain Bros., 2004.

Nicholas D. Kristof and Sheryl WuDunn   *Half the Sky: Turning Oppression into Opportunity for Women Worldwide*. New York: Alfred A. Knopf, 2009.

Marvin J. Levine   *Children for Hire: The Perils of Child Labor in the United States*. Westport, CT: Praeger Publishers, 2003.

Patricia McCormick   *Sold*. New York: Hyperion, 2006.

David L. Parker   *Before Their Time: The World of Child Labor*. New York: Quantuck Lane Press, 2007.

Robert J.S. Ross   *Slaves to Fashion: Poverty and Abuse in the New Sweatshops*. Ann Arbor, MI: University of Michigan Press, 2004.

Monica Feria
Tinta

The Landmark Rulings of the Inter-American Court of Human Rights on the Rights of the Child: Protecting the Most Vulnerable at the Edge. Boston: Martinus Nijhoff Publishers, 2008.

Michael D. Yates

Why Unions Matter. New York: Monthly Review Press, 2009.

Periodicals

Megha Bahree

"Child Labor," *Forbes*, February 25, 2008.

David Barboza

"Child Labor Rings Reach China's Distant Villages," *New York Times*, May 10, 2008.

Zoe Chafe

"Child Labor Harms Many Young Lives," Worldwatch Institute, www.WorldWatch.org, November 8, 2007.

E.R. Clough

"A Heartbreaking Visit to Child Labor Sweatshops," World of Good Development Organization, www.worldofgood.org, June 28, 2007.

Alan Delon

"Sweatshop Labor an Unfortunate Necessity in Third World," *Daily Cougar*, February 25, 2009.

Peter Dreier

"Human Rights Activists Protest NBA-Linked Sweatshops," www.CommonDreams.org, June 14, 2009.

Diane M. Grassi   "Free Trade Agreement with Oman Disregards Best Interests of U.S.," *American Chronicle*, July 5, 2006.

Steven Greenhouse   "Labor Fight Ends in Win for Students," *New York Times*, November 17, 2009.

Cheryl Grey   "Outsourcing: The Good Side of Asian Sweatshops," *Citizen Economists*, August 14, 2008.

Julia Hanna   "Why Sweatshops Flourish," *Harvard Business School Working Knowledge*, March 23, 2009.

Jaymi Heimbuch   "Fair Wage Guide Boosts Income for Women in Developing Nations," Planet Green, http://planetgreen.discovery.com, December 14, 2009.

International Program on the Elimination of Child Labour   "Give Girls a Chance. Tackling Child Labour, a Key to the Future," www.ilo.org, June 10, 2009.

Natasa Kovosevic   "Child Slavery: India's Self-Perpetuating Dilemma," *Harvard International Review*, Vol. 29, Summer 2007.

Nicholas D. Kristof   "Where Sweatshops Are a Dream," *New York Times*, January 14, 2009.

Shridhar Naik   "Child Labour—Legislation Alone Not Enough," www.Chowk.com, November 23, 2008.

Mary Nichols   "Child Labor and Economic Development: Making It Pay to Go to School," *Citizen Economists*, November 13, 2008.

Benjamin Powell   "In Defense of 'Sweatshops,'" *Library of Economics and Liberty*, June 2, 2008.

Benjamin Powell and David Skarbek   "Sweatshops and Third World Living Standards: Are the Jobs Worth the Sweat?" The Independent Institute, Working Paper #53, September 27, 2004.

Luke Pryor   "In Defense of Sweatshops," *Cornell Daily Sun*, October 27, 2009.

Rick Rousos   "Accident Highlights Child Care and Labor Law Issues," *The (Lakeland, FL) Ledger*, January 12, 2007.

Michael Strong   "Forget the World Bank, Try Wal-Mart," *ICS Daily*, August 22, 2006.

Daniel K. Tarullo   "A Sensible Approach to Labor Standards to Ensure Free Trade," Center for American Progress, March 2007.

Ian Urbina   "For Youths, a Grim Tour on Magazine Crews," *New York Times*, February 21, 2007.

Index